STATUS ANXIETY

STATUS
ANXIETY

Alain de Botton

HAMISH HAMILTON
an imprint of
PENGUIN BOOKS

HAMISH HAMILTON

Published by the Penguin Group

Penguin Books Ltd, 80 Strand, London WC2R 0RL, England

Penguin Group (USA) Inc., 375 Hudson Street, New York, New York 10014, USA

Penguin Books Australia Ltd, 250 Camberwell Road, Camberwell, Victoria 3214, Australia

Penguin Books Canada Ltd, 10 Alcorn Avenue, Toronto, Ontario, Canada M4V 3B2

Penguin Books India (P) Ltd, 11 Community Centre,

Panchsheel Park, New Delhi - 110 017, India

Penguin Books (NZ) Ltd, Cnr Rosedale and Airborne Roads,

Albany, Auckland, New Zealand

Penguin Books (South Africa) (Pty) Ltd, 24 Sturdee Avenue, Rosebank 2196, South Africa

Penguin Books Ltd, Registered Office: 80 Strand, London WC2R 0RL, England

www.penguin.com

First published 2004

1

Copyright © Alain de Botton, 2004

Set in 11/14.5 pt Minion

Designed by Austin Taylor

Printed in Great Britain by Butler & Tanner, Frome, Somerset

A CIP catalogue record for this book is available from the British Library

Hardback ISBN 0–241–14238– 5

Trade Paperback ISBN 0–241–14239–3

CONTENTS

CAUSES

I. Lovelessness 9

II. Snobbery 19

III. Expectation 31

IV. Meritocracy 65

V. Dependence 93

SOLUTIONS

I. Philosophy 113

II. Art 131

III. Politics 185

IV. Christianity 225

V. Bohemia 275

DEFINITIONS

Status

– One's position in society; the word derived from the Latin *statum* or standing (past participle of the verb *stare*, to stand).
– In a narrow sense, the word refers to one's legal or professional standing within a group (married, a lieutenant, etc.). But in the broader – and here more relevant – sense, to one's value and importance in the eyes of the world.
– Different societies have awarded status to different groups: hunters, fighters, ancient families, priests, knights, fecund women. Increasingly, since 1776, status in the West (the vague but comprehensible territory under discussion) has been awarded in relation to financial achievement.
– The consequences of high status are pleasant. They include resources, freedom, space, comfort, time and, as importantly perhaps, a sense of being cared for and thought valuable – conveyed through invitations, flattery, laughter (even when the joke lacks bite), deference and attention.
– High status is thought by many (but freely admitted by few) to be one of the finest of earthly goods.

Status Anxiety

– A worry, so pernicious as to be capable of ruining extended stretches of our lives, that we are in danger of failing to conform

to the ideals of success laid down by our society and that we may
as a result be stripped of dignity and respect; a worry that we are
currently occupying too modest a rung or are about to fall to a
lower one.

– The anxiety is provoked by, among other elements, recession,
redundancy, promotions, retirement, conversations with
colleagues in the same industry, newspaper profiles of the
prominent and the greater success of friends. Like confessing
to envy (to which the emotion is related), it can be socially
imprudent to reveal the extent of any anxiety and, therefore,
evidence of the inner drama is uncommon, limited usually to a
preoccupied gaze, a brittle smile or an over-extended pause
after news of another's achievement.

– If our position on the ladder is a matter of such concern, it is
because our self-conception is so dependent upon what others
make of us. Rare individuals aside (Socrates, Jesus), we rely on
signs of respect from the world to feel tolerable to ourselves.

– More regrettably still, status is hard to achieve and even harder
to maintain over a lifetime. Except in societies where it is fixed at
birth and our veins flow with noble blood, a high position hangs
on what we can achieve; and we may fail due to stupidity or an
absence of self-knowledge, macro-economics or malevolence.

– And from failure will flow humiliation: a corroding awareness that we have been unable to convince the world of our value and are henceforth condemned to consider the successful with bitterness and ourselves with shame.

Thesis

– That status anxiety possesses an exceptional capacity to inspire sorrow.

– That the hunger for status, like all appetites, can have its uses: spurring us to do justice to our talents, encouraging excellence, restraining us from harmful eccentricities and cementing members of a society around a common value system. But, like all appetites, its excesses can also kill.

– That the most profitable way of addressing the condition may be to attempt to understand and to speak of it.

PART ONE

CAUSES

I.
LOVELESSNESS

The Desire for Status

1

There are common assumptions about which motives drive us to seek high status; among them, a longing for money, fame and influence.

Alternatively, it might be more accurate to sum up what we are searching for with a word seldom used in political theory: love. Once food and shelter have been secured, the predominant impulse behind our desire to succeed in the social hierarchy may lie not so much with the goods we can accrue or the power we can wield, as with the amount of love we stand to receive as a consequence of high status. Money, fame and influence may be valued more as tokens of – and as a means to – love rather than as ends in themselves.

How might a word, generally used only in relation to what we would want from a parent or a romantic partner, be applied to something we might want from and be offered by the world? Perhaps we could define love, at once in its familial, sexual and worldly forms, as a kind of respect, a sensitivity by one person to another's existence. To be shown love is to feel ourselves the object of concern. Our presence is noted, our name is registered, our views are listened to, our failings are treated with indulgence and our needs are ministered to. And under such care, we flourish. There may be differences between romantic and status forms of love – the latter has no sexual dimension, it cannot end in marriage, those who offer it usually bear secondary motives – and yet those beloved in the status field will, just like romantic lovers, enjoy protection under the benevolent gaze of others.

It is common to describe people who hold important positions in society as 'somebodies' and their inverse as 'nobodies' – nonsensical terms, for we are all by necessity individuals with identities and comparable claims on existence. But such words are apt in conveying the variations in the quality of treatment meted out to different groups. Those without status remain unseen, they are treated brusquely, their complexities are trampled upon and their identities ignored.

The impact of low status should not be read in material terms alone. The penalty rarely lies, above subsistence levels at least, merely in physical discomfort. It lies also, and even primarily, in the challenge that low status poses to a sense of self-respect. Discomfort can be endured without complaint for long periods when it is unaccompanied by humiliation; as shown by the example of soldiers and explorers who have willingly endured privations that far exceeded those of the poorest in their societies, and yet who were sustained through their hardships by an awareness of the esteem they were held in by others.

The benefits of high status are similarly seldom limited to wealth. We should not be surprised to find many of the already affluent continuing to accumulate sums beyond anything that five generations might spend. Their endeavours are peculiar only if we insist on a strictly financial rationale behind wealth creation. As much as money, they seek the respect that stands to be derived from the process of gathering it. Few of us are determined aesthetes or sybarites, yet almost all of us hunger for dignity; and if a future society were to offer love as a reward for accumulating small plastic discs, then it would not be long before such worthless items too assumed a central place in our most zealous aspirations and anxieties.

2

Adam Smith, *The Theory of Moral Sentiments* (Edinburgh, 1759):
'To what purpose is all the toil and bustle of this world? What is the end of avarice and ambition, of the pursuit of wealth, of power and pre-eminence? Is it to supply the necessities of nature? The wages of the meanest labourer can supply them. What then are the advantages of that great purpose of human life which we call *bettering our condition*?

'To be observed, to be attended to, to be taken notice of with sympathy, complacency, and approbation, are all the advantages which we can propose to derive from it. The rich man glories in his riches because he feels that they naturally draw upon him the attention of the world. The poor man on the contrary is ashamed of his poverty. He feels that it places him out of the sight of mankind. To feel that we are taken no notice of necessarily disappoints the most ardent desires of human nature. The poor man goes out and comes in unheeded, and when in the midst of a crowd is in the same obscurity as if shut up in his own hovel. The man of rank and distinction, on the contrary, is observed by all the world. Everybody is eager to look at him. His actions are the objects of the public care. Scarce a word, scarce a gesture that fall from him will be neglected.'

3

Every adult life could be said to be defined by two great love stories. The first – the story of our quest for sexual love – is well known and well charted, its vagaries form the staple of music and literature, it is socially accepted and celebrated. The second – the story of our quest for love from the world – is a more secret and shameful tale. If mentioned, it tends to be in caustic, mocking terms, as something of interest chiefly to envious or deficient souls, or else the drive for status is interpreted in an economic sense alone. And yet this second love story is no less intense than the first, it is no less complicated, important or universal, and its setbacks are no less painful. There is heartbreak here too, suggested by the distant, resigned eyes of many whom the world has elected to dismiss as nobodies.

The Importance of Love

1

William James, *The Principles of Psychology* (Boston, 1890):
'No more fiendish punishment could be devised, were such a thing physically possible, than that one should be turned loose in society and remain absolutely unnoticed by all the members thereof. If no one turned around when we entered, answered when we spoke, or minded what we did, but if every person we met "cut us dead", and acted as if we were non-existent things, a kind of rage and impotent despair would before long well up in us, from which the cruellest bodily torture would be a relief.'

2

How are we affected by an absence of love? Why should being ignored drive us to a 'rage and impotent despair' beside which torture itself would be a relief?

The attentions of others might be said to matter to us principally because we are afflicted by a congenital uncertainty as to our own value – as a result of which what others think of us comes to play a determining role in how we are able to view ourselves. Our sense of identity is held captive by the judgements of those we live among. If they are amused by our jokes, we grow confident of our power to amuse. If they praise us, we develop an impression of high merit. And if they avoid our gaze as we enter a room or look impatient after we have revealed our occupation, we may fall into feelings of self-doubt and worthlessness.

We would, in an ideal world, be more impermeable. We would be unshaken whether we were ignored or noticed, praised or jeered at.

If someone fallaciously complimented us, we would not be unduly seduced. And if we had carried out a fair appraisal of ourselves and decided upon our value, another person's suggestion of our irrelevance would not wound us. We would know our worth. Instead, we appear to hold within ourselves a range of divergent views as to our characters. We have evidence of both cleverness and stupidity, humour and dullness, importance and superfluity. And in such wavering conditions, it typically falls to the attitude of society to settle the question of our significance. Neglect highlights our latent negative self-assessments, while a smile or compliment as rapidly brings out the converse. We seem beholden to the affections of others to endure ourselves.

Our 'ego' or self-conception could be pictured as a leaking balloon, forever requiring the helium of external love to remain inflated and vulnerable to the smallest pinpricks of neglect. There is something sobering and absurd in the extent to which we are cheered by attention and damage by disregard. Our mood may blacken because a colleague has greeted us absent-mindedly and our calls have been left unanswered. And we are capable of finding life worth living because someone has remembered our name and sent us a fruit basket.

3

It should not be surprising therefore if, from an emotional point of view no less than from a material one, we are anxious about the place we occupy in the world. This place will determine how much love we are offered and so, in turn, whether we can like or must lose confidence in ourselves. It holds the key to a commodity of unprecedented importance to us: a love without which we will be unable to trust or abide by our own characters.

The Consequences of Neglect

OTHERS' ATTITUDE	SELF-IMAGE
You are a failure	I am a disgrace
You are unimportant	I am a nobody
You are dim	I am stupid
	I am clever
	I am acceptable
	I am worthy

The Consequences of Love

OTHERS' ATTITUDE	SELF-IMAGE
You are intelligent	I am clever
You are important	I am acceptable
You are successful	I am worthy
	I am a disgrace
	I am a nobody
	I am stupid

II.
SNOBBERY

1

In our earliest years, no one minds much what we do, existence alone is enough to earn us unconditional affection. We can burp up our food, scream at the top of our voice, fail to earn any money and have no important friends – and still be valued.

But to reach adulthood means to take our place in a world dominated by chilling characters, snobs, whose behaviour lies at the heart of our anxieties about our status. Though certain friends and lovers will promise not to disown us even if we are bankrupted and disgraced (on a good day, we may even believe them), it is on a diet of the highly conditional attentions of snobs that we are generally forced to subsist.

2

The word 'snobbery' came into use for the first time in England during the 1820s. It was said to have derived from the habit of many Oxford and Cambridge colleges of writing *sine nobilitate* (without nobility) or '*s.nob.*' next to the names of ordinary students on examination lists in order to distinguish them from their aristocratic peers.

In the word's earliest days, a snob was taken to mean someone without high status, but it quickly assumed its modern and almost diametrically opposed meaning: someone offended by a lack of high status in others. It was also clear that those who used the word were doing so pejoratively, to describe a process of discrimination they found regrettable and worthy of mockery. In his *Book of Snobs* (1848), a pioneering essay on the subject, William Thackeray observed that snobs had, over the previous twenty-five years, 'spread over England like the railroads. They are now known and recognized throughout an Empire on which the sun never sets.' But, in truth, what was new was not snobbery, but a spirit of equality beside which a traditional kind of discriminatory conduct now seemed increasingly unacceptable, to men like Thackeray at least.

3

Since then, it has grown common to describe as a snob almost anyone who practises overt social or cultural bias, who declares one kind of person or music or wine to be plainly better than another. Snobs comprise – according to this understanding – all those who insist too loudly on a scale of values.

Yet it might be more accurate to limit the meaning of snobbery to a particular way of resolving the question of who and what to respect. The distinctive mark of snobs is not simple discrimination, it is an insistence on a flawless equation between social rank and human worth.

Though traditionally they may have been associated with an interest in the aristocracy (for they were first pinned down in language at a time and place when aristocrats stood at the apex of society), the identification of snobbery with an enthusiasm for hunting and gentlemen's clubs hardly captures the diversity of the phenomenon. Snobs can through time be found ingratiating themselves with a range of prominent groups – soldiers (Sparta, 400 BC), bishops (Rome, 1500), poets (Weimar, 1815), farmers (China, 1967) – for the primary interest of snobs is power, and as the distribution of power changes, so, naturally and immediately, will the objects of their admiration.

4

The company of the snobbish has the power to enrage and unnerve because we sense how little of who we are deep down – that is, how little of who we are outside of our status – will be able to govern their behaviour towards us. We may be endowed with the wisdom of Solomon and have the resourcefulness and intelligence of Odysseus, but if we are unable to wield socially recognized badges of our qualities, our existence will remain a matter of raw indifference to them.

This conditional nature perhaps pains us because adult love retains as its prototype the unconditional love of a parent for a child. Our earliest experience of love is of being cared for in a naked, impoverished condition. Babies cannot, by definition, repay their carers with worldly rewards. In so far as they are loved and looked after, it is therefore for who they are – identity in its barest, most stripped-down state. They are loved for, or in spite of, their uncontrolled, howling and stubborn characters.

Only as we mature does affection begin to depend on achievement: being polite, succeeding at school and later, acquiring rank and prestige. Such efforts may attract the interest of others, but the underlying emotional craving may not be so much to dazzle because of our deeds as to recapture the tenor of the bountiful, indiscriminate petting we received in return for arranging wooden bricks on the kitchen floor, for having a soft, plump body and wide trusting eyes.

It is evidence of this craving that only the most inept flatterer would admit to a wish to base a friendship around an attraction to power or fame. Such assets would feel like insulting and volatile reasons to be invited to lunch, for they lie outside the circle of our true and irreducible selves. Jobs can be lost and influence eroded without us perishing nor our childhood-founded need for affection slackening. Talented flatterers therefore know they should suggest that it is strictly the status-less part of their prey they are interested

in, that the ambassadorial car, newspaper profiles or company direc-
torship are mere coincidental features of a profound and pure
attachment.

Yet, despite their efforts, the prey are liable to detect the fickleness
beneath the polished surface and leave the company of snobs fearing
the irrelevance of their essential selves beside any status which, for a
time, they may hold precariously in their hands.

5

Given their exclusive interest in reputation and achievement, when
the outer circumstances of their acquaintances alter, snobs are prone
to make some sudden tragicomic reassessments of who their closest
friends might be.

One foggy evening in Paris at the end of the nineteenth century,
the bourgeois narrator of Marcel Proust's *In Search of Lost Time*
(1922) travels to an expensive restaurant to have dinner with an
aristocratic friend, the Marquis de Saint-Loup. He arrives early,
Saint-Loup is late and the staff, judging their client on the basis of a
shabby coat and an unfamiliar name, assume that a nobody has
entered their establishment. They therefore patronize him, take him
to a table around which an arctic draught is blowing and are slow to
offer him anything to drink or eat.

But, a quarter of an hour later, the marquis arrives, identifies his
friend and at a stroke transforms the narrator's value in the eyes of
the staff. The manager bows deeply before him, draws out the menu,
recites the specials of the day with evocative flourishes, compliments
him on his clothes and, so as to prevent him thinking that these
courtesies are in any way dependent on his link to an aristocrat,
occasionally gives him a surreptitious little smile which seems to
indicate a wholly personal affection. When the narrator asks him for
some bread, the manager clicks his heels and exclaims:

'"Certainly, Monsieur le baron!" "I am not a baron," I told him in a tone of mock sadness. "Oh, I beg your pardon, Monsieur le comte!" I had no time to lodge a second protest, which would no doubt have promoted me to the rank of marquis.'

However satisfactory the volte-face, the underlying dynamic is bleak, for the manager has not of course amended his snobbish value-system in any way. He has merely rewarded someone differently within its brutal confines – and only rarely do we have the opportunity to find a Marquis de Saint-Loup or a Prince Charming who can speak on our behalf to convince the world of the nobility of our souls. We are more commonly made to finish our dinner in the arctic draught.

6

The problem is compounded by newspapers. Because snobs combine a weak capacity for independent judgement with an appetite for the views of influential people, their beliefs will, to a critical degree, be set by the atmosphere of the press.

Thackeray proposed that the obsessive English concern with high status and aristocracy could be traced back to the country's papers, which daily enforced messages about the prestige of the titled and the famous and, by implication, the banality of the untitled and the ordinary. His particular bugbear was the 'Court Circular' section of the papers, which reverently covered the parties, holidays, births and deaths of 'high society'. On selected days in October 1848, the month of publication of his *Book of Snobs*, the Court Circular of the *Morning Post* reported on Lord Brougham's hunting party at Brougham Hall ('a good sport was had by all'), Lady Agnes Duff's impending accouchement in Edinburgh and Georgina Pakenham's marriage to Lord Burghley ('Her Ladyship was magnificently attired in a white satin dress, with lace flounces and a corsage montant. It is needless to say that she looked exquisite').

'How can you help being snobs, so long as this balderdash is set before you?' wondered Thackeray. 'Oh, down with the papers, those engines and propagators of Snobbishness!' And, to expand on Thackeray's thought, how greatly the levels of status anxiety might diminish if only the newspapers were to exchange a fraction of their interest in Lady Agnes Duff and her successors for a focus on the significance of ordinary life.

7

To try to understand the problem, it is perhaps only ever fear that is to blame. Belittling others is no pastime for those convinced of their own standing. There is terror behind haughtiness. It takes a punishing impression of our own inferiority to leave others feeling that they aren't good enough for us.

The fear flows down the generations. In a pattern common to all abusive behaviour, snobs generate snobs. An older generation inflicts its own unusually powerful association between modest rank and catastrophe, denying its offspring the layer of emotional bedding that would grant them the inner ease to imagine that low status (their own and that of others) does not neatly equate with unworthiness, nor high status with excellence.

'There go the Spicer Wilcoxes, Mamma!' a daughter exclaims to her mother while walking in Hyde Park on a spring morning in a *Punch* cartoon of 1892. 'I'm told they're dying to know us. Hadn't we better call?'

'Certainly not, dear,' replies the mother. 'If they're dying to know us, they're not worth knowing. The only people worth *our* knowing are the people who *don't* want to know us!'

Unless Mamma can be helped to heal the scars to which her

"THERE GO THE SPICER WILCOXES, MAMMA! I'M TOLD THEY'RE DYING TO KNOW US. HADN'T WE BETTER CALL?"
"CERTAINLY NOT, DEAR. IF THEY'RE DYING TO KNOW US, THEY'RE NOT WORTH KNOWING. THE ONLY PEOPLE WORTH *OUR* KNOWING ARE THE PEOPLE WHO DON'T WANT TO KNOW US!"

behaviour testifies, there is little hope that she will ever be capable of a more rounded interest in the Spicer Wilcoxes – and so little hope that the cycles of fear-induced snobbery will ever be interrupted.

Yet it is hard to renounce snobbish tactics on our own, for the disease is a collective one to begin with. A youthful resentment of snobbery isn't enough to save us from gradually turning into snobs ourselves, because being insolently neglected almost naturally fosters a hunger to gain the attention of our neglectors (disliking people rarely being a sufficient reason for not wanting *them* to like *us*). The snobbery of a prominent group can thereby draw the population as a whole towards social ambitions that it may initially have had no taste for but now pursues as the only apparent means to love and recognition.

Rather than scorn, sorrow and understanding might be more accurate responses to behaviour motivated at heart by a frightened and frustrated desire for dignity.

It may be tempting to laugh at those afflicted by urgent cravings for the symbols of status: the name-droppers, the gold-tap owners. The history of Victorian furniture was dominated by the sale of some candidly tasteless items. Many of them were the work of the London firm of Jackson & Graham whose most flamboyant offering was a carved cabinet of pollard oak, decked out with figures of boys gathering grapes, two female caryatids and a set of carved pilasters. The whole was crowned by a majestic 60-centimetre-high gold-plated bull.

Before mocking anyone who bought such a piece, it would perhaps be fairer to wonder about the wider context in which this kind of furniture was made and consumed. Rather than teasing the buyers, we may blame the society in which they lived for setting up a situation where the purchase of ornate cabinets felt psychologically necessary and rewarding, where respect was dependent on baroque displays. Rather than a tale of greed, the history of luxury could more accurately be read as a record of emotional trauma. It is the legacy of those who have felt pressured by the disdain of others to add an extraordinary amount to their bare selves in order to signal that they too may lay a claim to love.

8

If poverty is the customary material penalty for low status, then neglect and faraway looks will be the emotional penalties that a snobbish world appears unable to stop imposing on those bereft of the symbols of importance.

Carved cabinet of pollard oak, Jackson & Graham, London, 1852

III.
EXPECTATION

Nikita Khrushchev and Richard Nixon outside the kitchen of the 'Taj Mahal', the American National Exhibition, Moscow, 1959

Material Progress

1

In July 1959, the American vice-president, Richard Nixon, travelled to Moscow to open an exhibition showcasing his country's techno- logical and material achievements. The highlight of the exhibition was a full-scale replica of the home of an average American worker: it was equipped with fitted carpets, a television in the living room, two en suite bathrooms, central heating and a kitchen with a wash- ing machine, a tumble-dryer and a refrigerator.

Reporting on the exhibition, an incensed Soviet press angrily denied that an ordinary American worker could conceivably live in such luxury and advised its readers to dismiss the entire house as a piece of propaganda – after mockingly baptizing it the 'Taj Mahal'.

When Nixon led Nikita Khrushchev around the exhibition, the Soviet leader was comparably sceptical. Outside the kitchen of the model home, Khrushchev spotted an electric lemon squeezer and remarked to Nixon that no one in their right mind would want to acquire such a 'silly gadget'.

'Anything that makes women work less hard must be useful,' answered Nixon.

'We don't think of women in terms of workers – like you do in the capitalist system,' snapped back an irate Khrushchev.

Later that evening, Nixon was invited to make a broadcast on Soviet television, and used the occasion to expound on the ad- vantages of American life. Shrewdly, he did not begin his speech by mentioning democracy or human rights; he started with money and material progress. Nixon explained that Western countries had, through enterprise and industry, in just a few hundred years, managed to overcome the poverty and famine that had existed up to the middle of the eighteenth century – and which still continued in many parts of the world. Modern Americans owned 56 million television sets and 143 million radios, he informed his Soviet audience, many of whom lacked access to their own bathroom or kettle. Some 31 million families had bought their own homes. The average American family could buy 9 dresses and suits and 14 pairs of shoes every year. In the United States, one could get a house in a thousand different architectural styles. Most of these houses were larger than a television studio. An infuriated Khrushchev sat at Nixon's side, clenched his fists and mouthed, 'Nyet! Nyet!' – adding under his breath, according to one account, 'Ëb' tvoyu babushky.' (Go fuck your grandmother.)

2

But Nixon wasn't lying. In the two centuries that preceded his speech, the countries of the West had witnessed the fastest, most radical transformation in living standards ever known in history.

The majority of the population of medieval and early modern Europe had belonged to the peasant class. They had been poor, undernourished, cold, fearful and dead – usually following some agony – before their fortieth birthdays. After a lifetime of work, their most expensive possession might have been a cow, a goat or a pot. Famine had never been far away and diseases had been rife; among the most common were rickets, ulcers, tuberculosis, leprosy, abscesses, gangrene, tumours and cankers.

3

Then, in early eighteenth-century Britain, the great Western transformation began. Thanks to new farming techniques (crop rotation, scientific stock-breeding and land-consolidation), agricultural yields began to rise sharply. From 1700 to 1820, Britain's agricultural productivity doubled, releasing capital and manpower that flowed into the cities and was invested in industry and trade. The invention of the steam engine and the cotton power-loom altered working practices and social expectations. Towns exploded in size. In 1800, only one city in the British Isles, London, had a population of over a hundred thousand. By 1891, there were twenty-three such cities. Goods and services that had formerly been the preserve of an elite became widely available. Luxuries became decencies, and decencies necessities. Daniel Defoe, travelling around southern England in 1745, noticed the opening of large new shops with enticing window displays and products. Whereas, for much of recorded history, fashion had remained static for decades or more, it grew possible to identify specific styles for every passing year (in England in 1753 purple was in vogue for women, in 1754 it was the turn of white linen with a pink pattern and in 1755 of dove grey).

The British consumer revolution spread and expanded in the nineteenth century. Giant new department stores opened throughout Europe and America: the Bon Marché and Au Printemps in Paris, Selfridge's and Whiteley's in London, Macy's in New York.

They offered ordinary people goods that previously had been the preserve of royalty. At the ribbon-cutting ceremony to mark the opening of a new twelve-storey Marshall Field's in Chicago in 1902, the manager, Gordon Selfridge, explained that, 'We have built this great institution for ordinary people, so that it can be their store, their downtown home, their buying headquarters.' It was not, he said, just for the 'swagger rich'.

A host of technological inventions transformed everyday life – and helped to alter mental horizons too: the old cyclical view of the world, where one expected next year to be much like (and as bad as) the last, gave way to a view that mankind could progress yearly towards perfection. To list only a few of these inventions:

Central staircase, Bon Marché department store, Paris, 1880

Cornflakes were patented by J. H. Kellogg in 1895, after he had hit upon the concept by accident when the grain mixture he served the inmates in his sanatorium had hardened by mistake and been shattered into flakes.

The **can-opener** was patented in 1870.

The **safetypin** was invented in 1849.

The **sewing machine** was developed by I. M. Singer in 1851. Ready-made clothes started to become more common from the 1860s; machine-made underclothes appeared in the 1870s.

The **typewriter** was invented in 1867 (the first manuscript to be typed was Mark Twain's *Life on the Mississippi* in 1883).

Processed foods: By the 1860s, Britain's Crosse & Blackwell was manufacturing twenty-seven thousand gallons of ketchup a year. In the early 1880s, the chemist Alfred Bird invented an egg-less custard powder. Blancmange powder was invented in the 1870s and jelly crystals in the 1890s.

Lighting: Stearic candles were used from the 1830s, replacing the much shorter-lived tallow-dip candles of old.

Sanitation: In 1846, Doulton began manufacturing glazed stoneware pipes which created a revolution in metropolitan sewerage. By the late 1870s, public toilets began to appear in Europe and America. George Jennings's famous 'pedestal vase' of 1884 stunned the public by its ability to wash away, as its advertisement put it, 'ten apples and a flat sponge with a two-gallon flush'.

The **telephone** was invented by Alexander Graham Bell in 1863.

Dry-cleaning was invented in 1849 by the Parisian tailor Jolly-Bellin who had accidentally spilt turpentine on to a tablecloth and found that the patch it had covered had been cleared of stains. From 1866, Pullars of Perth was offering a postal two-day dry-cleaning service anywhere in the British Isles and had improved on Jolly-Bellin's cleaning fluid with a mixture of petroleum and benzene.

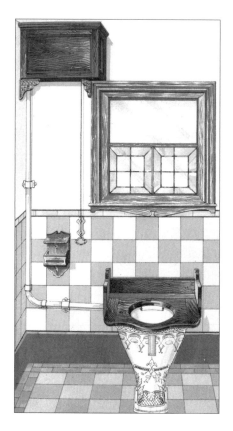

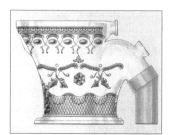

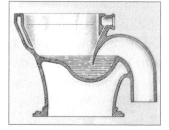

George Jennings, pedestal vase, 1884

4

Material progress accelerated still further in the twentieth century. In his *English Journey* (1934), J. B. Priestley observed that a new kind of England had taken shape, a country of arterial roads and bungalows, where ordinary workers read tabloid newspapers, listened to the radio, spent their leisure hours shopping and looked forward to rising incomes year by year: 'In this England, for the first time, Jack and Jill are nearly as good as their master and mistress.'

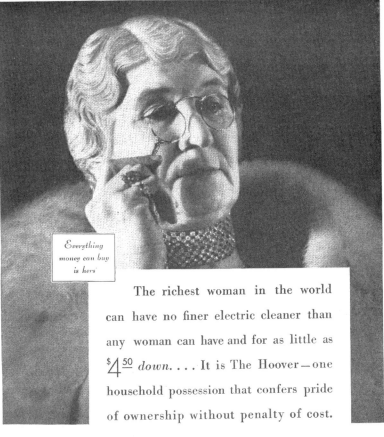

The richest woman in the world can have no finer electric cleaner than any woman can have and for as little as $4 $\frac{50}{}$ *down.* . . . It is The Hoover — one household possession that confers pride of ownership without penalty of cost.

The new and exclusive Hoover Hedlite makes cleaning easy in darkest corners.

Of no other cleaner can this be said: More homes— mansions or cottages—are cleaned by Hoovers than by any other cleaner. . . . *Hoover is the oldest* maker of electric cleaners and the largest. *More than 3,000,000* Hoovers have been sold. . . . The Hoover is *unique* due to its exclusive, patented cleaning principle, Positive Agitation. By gently beating the rug, The Hoover dislodges even the most deeply embedded grit so injurious to rugs, and removes it along with lint, hair, litter and dust. . . . It is recommended by leading rug manufacturers for the cleaning and care of floor coverings. . . . *The Hoover* is not only more efficient at the start, but is kept efficient by its sturdier construction. . . . *The Hoover, complete with Dusting Tools or Dustette, may be bought on as low a down* payment and with as small an outlay per month as the cheapest machine, yet a Hoover brings you many more years of cleaning service. . . . *The Hoover is sold* and endorsed by the leading merchants of the country. Open your door with confidence to their bonded and trustworthy representatives. . . . The Hoover man will be glad to leave any of the three new Hoovers for a no-obligation home trial. *The Hoover Co. Factories: North Canton, Ohio; Hamilton, Ontario.*

The HOOVER
It Beats . . . as it Sweeps . . . as it Cleans

A democratic consumer revolution: Hoover advertisement, February 1933

In *The Lion and the Unicorn* (1941), George Orwell sketched similar facets of the Western material revolution: 'Nearly all citizens of civilized countries now enjoy the use of good roads, germ-free water, police protection, free libraries and probably free education of a kind. To an increasing extent the rich and the poor read the same books, and they also see the same films and listen to the same radio programmes. The differences in their way of life have been diminished by the mass-production of cheap clothes and improvements in housing. The place to look for the germs of the future England is in light-industry areas and along the arterial roads. In Slough, Dagenham, Barnet, Letchworth, Hayes – everywhere, indeed, on the outskirts of great towns – the old pattern is gradually changing into something new. In those vast new wildernesses of glass and brick, there is a rather restless, culture-less life, centring round tinned food, *Picture Post*, the radio and the internal combustion engine.'

When Franklin D. Roosevelt was asked what book he could give the Soviets to teach them about the advantages of American society, he pointed to the Sears catalogue.

In the economic expansion that followed the Second World War, Western, and in particular American, consumers became the most privileged, and most harried, on the planet.

Across the United States new longings were created by the development of malls, which enabled citizens to shop at all hours in climate-controlled environments. When the Southdale mall opened in Minnesota in 1950, its advertising announced that, 'Every day will be a perfect shopping day at Southdale.'

By the 1970s, Americans were estimated to be spending more time at the mall than anywhere else – besides their workplaces and their Taj Mahals.

Sears catalogue, spring 1934

Andreas Gursky, 99 cents, 2000

Equality, Expectation and Envy

1

The advantages of two thousand years of Western civilization are familiar enough: an extraordinary increase in wealth, in food supply, in scientific knowledge, in consumer goods, in physical security, in life expectancy and economic opportunity. What is perhaps less apparent and more perplexing is the way that such impressive material advances may have gone hand in hand with a phenomenon left unmentioned in Nixon's address to his Soviet audience: a rise in levels of status anxiety among ordinary Western citizens, by which is meant a rise in levels of concern about importance, achievement and income.

A sharp decline in *actual* deprivation may – paradoxically – have been accompanied by a continuing and even increased *sense* of deprivation and a fear of it. Populations blessed with riches and possibilities far outstripping those imaginable by their ancestors tilling the unpredictable soil of medieval Europe have shown a remarkable capacity to feel that both who they are and what they have are not enough.

2

These feelings of deprivation may not look so peculiar, however, once we consider the psychology behind the way we decide what is enough. Our sense of an appropriate limit to anything – for example, to wealth and esteem – is never decided independently. It is arrived at by comparing our condition with that of a reference group, with that of people we consider to be our equals. We cannot appreciate what we have in isolation, or judged against the lives of our medieval forebears. We cannot be impressed by how prosperous we are in historical terms. We will take ourselves to be fortunate only when we have as much as, or a little more than, the people we grow up with, work alongside, have as friends and identify with in the public realm.

If we are made to live in a draughty, insalubrious cottage and bend to the harsh rule of an aristocrat in command of a large and well-heated castle, and yet we observe that all our equals live as we do, then our condition will seem normal; regrettable, certainly, but not fertile ground for a sense of envy. If we have a pleasant home and comfortable job, however, but learn through ill-advised attendance at a school reunion that some of our old friends (there is no stronger reference group) are now living in houses larger than our own, bought on the proceeds of more enticing occupations, we are likely to return home nursing a violent sense of misfortune.

It is the feeling that we might be something other than what we are – a feeling transmitted by the superior achievements of those we take to be our equals – that generates anxiety and resentment. If we are small and live among people who are all of own height, we will not be unduly troubled by questions of size (Figure 1).

Figure 1

But if others in our group grow so much as a little taller, we are liable to feel sudden unease and fall into dissatisfaction and envy – even though we have not ourselves diminished in size by even a millimetre (Figure 2).

Figure 2

Given the vast inequalities we are daily confronted with, perhaps the most notable feature of envy is that we manage not to envy everyone. There are people whose enormous blessings leave us wholly untroubled, others whose minor advantages act as sources of relentless torment. We envy only those whom we feel ourselves to be like; we envy only members of our reference group. There are few successes more unendurable than those of our close friends.

3
David Hume, *A Treatise on Human Nature* (Edinburgh, 1739):
'It is not a great disproportion between ourselves and others which produces envy, but on the contrary, a proximity. A common soldier bears no envy for his general compared to what he will feel for his sergeant or corporal; nor does an eminent writer meet with as much jealousy in common hackney scribblers, as in authors that more nearly approach him. A great disproportion cuts off the relation, and either keeps us from comparing ourselves with what is remote from us or diminishes the effects of the comparison.'

4
It follows that the more people we take to be our equals and compare ourselves to, the more people there will be to envy.

In so far as the great political and consumer revolutions of the eighteenth and nineteenth centuries led to psychological anguish even as they vastly improved the material lot of mankind, it is because of an extraordinary new ideal around which they were founded: a practical belief in the innate equality of all humans and in the unlimited power of anyone to achieve anything.

For most of history an opposite assumption had held sway: inequality and low expectations had been viewed as both normal and wise. Only a very few had ever aspired to wealth and fulfilment. The majority knew well enough that they were condemned to exploitation and resignation.

'It is clear that some men are by nature free and others are by nature slaves, and that for these latter, slavery is both expedient and right,' Aristotle had declared in his *Politics* (350 BC) – to the approval of almost all Greek and Roman thinkers and leaders. In the ancient world, slaves and the working classes generally had been considered creatures lacking in reason, and therefore naturally fitted to dismal lives, as beasts of burden were to tilling fields. To hold that they might have rights and aspirations would have been thought by the elite to be no less absurd than to enquire into the mental state and level of happiness of a hammer or scythe.

The notion that inequality was fair or at least irrevocable was often shared by the oppressed themselves. With the spread of Christian teachings during the later Roman Empire, many fell prey to a religion that taught them to interpret their unequal treatment as part of a natural, unchangeable order. Despite the egalitarian principles within Christ's teachings, there was little suggestion from Christian political theorists that the earthly social structure could be reformed in order for members to share more fairly in the wealth of the land. Humans might be equal before God, but this offered no reason to start seeking equality in practice.

For these theorists, a good Christian society therefore took the form of a rigidly stratified absolute monarchy, which was said to reflect the ordering of the celestial kingdom. Just as God wielded absolute power over all creation, from the angels down to the smallest toads, so too his appointed rulers on earth were understood to preside over a society where God had given everyone his and her place, from the nobleman down to the farmhand. To have accused a medieval English aristocrat of 'snobbery' for his attitudes to those below him in the hierarchy would have made no sense. A derogatory

A medieval vision of hierarchy: Jacobello de Fiore,
The Coronation of the Virgin in Paradise, *1438*

term for segregation could make an appearance only once a more egalitarian way of looking at people had come to seem a possibility.

Sir John Fortescue, the English fifteenth-century jurist, was repeating an idea taken for granted throughout the medieval period when he explained, 'From the highest angel down to the lowest, there is no angel that is without both a superior and inferior; nor from man down to the meanest worm is there any creature which is not in some respect superior to one creature and inferior to another.' To challenge why certain people were condemned to till the soil while others feasted in banqueting halls was, for the dominant ideology, to challenge the Creator's will.

In his *Policraticus* (1159), John of Salisbury became the most famous Christian writer to compare society to a body – and to use the analogy to justify a system of natural inequality. In Salisbury's account, every part of the state could be likened to part of a human being: the ruler was the head, the parliament was the heart, the court were the sides, the officers and judges were the eyes, ears and tongue, the belly and intestines were the treasury, armies were the hands and the peasants and workers were the feet. The image suggested that everyone in society had been allotted an unalterable role and that it would have been as peculiar for a peasant to request to take up residence in a manor-house and have a say in government as for a toe to want to be an eye.

5

It was not until the middle of the seventeenth century that political thinking began to edge in a more egalitarian direction.

In his *Leviathan* (1651), Thomas Hobbes proposed that individuals had existed prior to the birth of societies and had joined these societies only for their own benefit, agreeing to surrender their natural rights in exchange for protection – a seminal point repeated a few decades later by John Locke in his *Two Treatises of Government* (1689). God had not, reasoned Locke, given Adam 'private dominion' over the earth, he had given it 'to mankind in common' for the enjoyment of everyone. Rulers were the instruments of the people and were fit to be obeyed only in so far as they served the general interest. An astonishing modern idea was born: that the justification of governments lies in their ability to promote opportunities for prosperity and happiness among all those they rule over.

Calls for political equality and social and economic opportunity that had been in the ether for a century and a half finally found dramatic, concrete expression in the American Revolution of 1776. Perhaps more so than any other event in Western history (more than the French Revolution that succeeded it), this revolution changed for ever the basis upon which status was accorded, shifting societies from hereditary aristocratic hierarchies, where there were limited opportunities for advancement and where status was ascribed on the basis of the age and distinction of one's family, to dynamic economies, where status was ascribed according to the (largely financial) achievements of each new generation.

By 1791, the geographer Jedidiah Morse was writing of New England that it was a place 'where every man thinks himself at least as good as his neighbours, and believes that all mankind have, or ought to possess, equal rights'. American etiquette evolved in a democratic direction. Servants ceased calling their employers 'master' or 'mistress'. The titles 'Esquire' and 'His Honour' were banned. All American states abolished primogeniture and equal property rights were given to daughters and widows. The physician and historian David Ramsay, in his *Oration on the Advantages of American Independence* delivered on 4 July 1778, explained that the goal of the revolution was to create a society where 'all offices lie open to men of merit of whatever rank or condition. Even the reins of state may be held by the son of the poorest man, if he is possessed of abilities that are equal to this important station.' In his auto-biography, Thomas Jefferson explained that his life had been directed towards creating 'an opening for the aristocracy of virtue and talent', to replace the old aristocracy of privilege and, in many cases, brute stupidity.

In his *Leaves of Grass* (1855), Walt Whitman identified the greatness of America with equality and lack of deference: 'The genius of the United States is not best or most in its executives or legislatures, nor in its ambassadors or authors or colleges or churches or parlours, nor even in its newspapers and inventors ... but always most in the common people ... the air they have of persons who never knew how it felt to stand in the presence of superiors ... the terrible significance of their elections – the President's taking off his hat to them not they to him ...'

6

But even admirers of consumer and democratic revolutions could not help but notice a particular problem visited upon the modern equal societies they created. One of the first thinkers to dwell on it was Alexis de Tocqueville.

Travelling around the young United States in the 1830s, the French lawyer and historian discerned an unexpected ill corroding the souls of the citizens of the new republic. Americans had much, but this affluence did not stop them from wanting ever more and from suffering whenever they saw someone else with assets they lacked. In a chapter of *Democracy in America* (1835) entitled 'Why the Americans are Often so Restless in the Midst of Their Prosperity', he sketched an enduring analysis of the relationship between dissatis-faction and high expectation, between envy and equality:

'When all the prerogatives of birth and fortune have been abolished, when every profession is open to everyone, an ambitious man may think it is easy to launch himself on a great career and feel that he has been called to no common destiny. But this is a delusion which experience quickly corrects. When inequality is the general rule in society, the greatest inequalities attract no attention. But when everything is more or less level, the slightest variation is noticed ... That is the reason for the strange melancholy often haunting inhabitants of democracies in the midst of abundance and for that disgust with life sometimes gripping them even in calm and easy circumstances. In France, we are worried about the increasing rate of suicides. In America, suicide is rare, but I am told that madness is commoner than anywhere else.'

Familiar with the limitations of aristocratic societies, Tocqueville had no wish to return to the conditions that had existed prior to 1776 or 1789. He knew that inhabitants of the modern West enjoyed a standard of living far superior to that of the lower classes of medieval Europe. Nevertheless, he appreciated that these deprived classes had also benefited from a mental calm which their successors were forever denied:

'When royal power supported by aristocracies governed nations, society, despite all its wretchedness, enjoyed several types of happiness which are difficult to appreciate today. Having never conceived the possibility of a social state other than the one they knew, and never expecting to become equal to their leaders, the people did not question their rights. They felt neither repugnance nor degradation in sub-mitting to severities, which seemed to them like inevitable ills sent by God. The serf considered his inferiority as an effect of the immutable order of nature. Consequently, a sort of goodwill was established between classes so differently favoured by fortune. One found in-equality in society, but men's souls were not degraded thereby.'

Democracies, however, had dismantled every barrier to expecta-tion. All members of the community felt themselves theoretically equal, even when they lacked the means to achieve material equality.

'In America,' wrote Tocqueville, 'I never met a citizen too poor to cast a glance of hope and envy toward the pleasures of the rich.' Poor citizens observed rich ones at close quarters and trusted that they too would one day follow in their footsteps. They were not always wrong. A number of fortunes were made by people from humble backgrounds. However, exceptions did not make a rule. America still had an underclass. It was just that, unlike the poor of aristocratic societies, the American poor were no longer able to see their condition as anything other than a betrayal of their expectations.

The different conceptions of poverty held by members of aristocratic and of democratic societies were particularly evident, Tocqueville felt, in the attitude of servants to their masters. In aristocracies, servants often accepted their fates with good grace; they could have, in Tocqueville's words, 'high thoughts, strong pride and self-respect'. In democracies, however, the atmosphere of the press and public opinion relentlessly suggested to servants that they could reach the pinnacles of society, that they could become industrialists, judges, scientists or presidents. Though this sense of unlimited opportunity could initially encourage a surface cheerfulness, especially in young servants, and though it enabled the most talented or lucky among them to fulfil their goals, as time passed and the majority failed to raise themselves, Tocqueville noted that their mood darkened, that bitterness took hold and choked their spirits, and that their hatred of themselves and their masters grew fierce.

The rigid hierarchical system that had held in place in almost every Western society until the eighteenth century, and had denied all hope of social movement except in rare cases, the system glorified by John of Salisbury and John Fortescue, was unjust in a thousand all too obvious ways, but it offered those on the lowest rungs one notable freedom: the freedom not to have to take the achievements of quite so many people in society as reference points – and so find themselves severely wanting in status and importance as a result.

7

It was an American himself, William James, who, a few decades after Tocqueville's journey around the United States, explored from a psychological angle the problem created by societies which generate unlimited expectations in their members.

For James, satisfaction with ourselves does not require us to succeed in every area of endeavour. We are not always humiliated by failing at things; we are humiliated only if we first invest our pride and sense of worth in a given achievement, and then do not reach it. Our goals determine what we will interpret as a triumph and what must count as a failure. James, a professor of psychology at Harvard, had invested his pride in being a prominent psychologist. Therefore, if others knew more psychology than he did, he would, he admitted, feel envy and shame. However, because he had never set himself the task of learning ancient Greek, that someone could translate the whole of the *Symposium* whereas he struggled with the opening line was a matter of no concern.

'With no attempt there can be no failure and with no failure no humiliation. So our self-esteem in this world depends entirely on what we *back* ourselves to be and do. It is determined by the ratio of our actualities to our supposed potentialities. Thus:

$$\text{Self-esteem} \ = \ \frac{\text{Success}}{\text{Pretensions}}\text{'}$$

James's equation illustrates how every rise in our levels of expectation entails a rise in the dangers of humiliation. What we understand to be normal is critical in determining our chances of happiness. Few things rival the torment of the once-famous actor, the fallen politician or, as Tocqueville might have remarked, the unsuccessful American.

The equation also hints at two manoeuvres for raising our self-esteem. On the one hand, we may try to achieve more; and on the other, we may reduce the number of things we want to achieve. James pointed to the advantages of the latter approach:

'To give up pretensions is as blessed a relief as to get them gratified. There is a strange lightness in the heart when one's nothingness in a particular area is accepted in good faith. How pleasant is the day when we give up striving to be young or slender. "Thank God!" we say, "*those* illusions are gone." Everything added to the self is a burden as well as a pride.'

8

Unfortunately for our self-esteem, societies of the West are not known for their conduciveness to the surrender of pretensions, to the acceptance of age or fat, let alone poverty and obscurity. Their mood urges us to invest ourselves in activities and belongings that our predecessors would have had no thought of. According to James's equation, by greatly increasing our pretensions, these societies render adequate self-esteem almost impossible to secure.

The dangers of disappointed expectation must further be increased by any erosion of a faith in a next world. Those who can believe that what happens on earth is but a brief prelude to an eternal existence will offset any tendency to envy with the thought that the success of others is a momentary phenomenon against the backdrop of an eternal life.

But when a belief in a next world is interpreted as a childish and scientifically impossible opiate, the pressure to succeed and fulfil oneself will inevitably be inflamed by the awareness that there is only a single and frighteningly brief opportunity to do so. Earthly achievements can no longer be seen as an overture to what one may realize in another world, they are the sum total of all one will ever be.

A firm belief in the necessary misery of life was for centuries one of mankind's most important assets, a bulwark against bitterness, one cruelly undermined by the expectations incubated by the modern world-view. In his *City of God* (AD 427), St Augustine had consolingly described unhappiness as an immovable feature of existence, part of 'the wretchedness of man's situation', and had poured scorn on 'all those theories by which men have tried hard to build up joy for themselves within the misery of this life'. Under Augustine's influence, the French poet Eustache Deschamps (*c.*1338–1410) had written of life on earth as a:

> Time of mourning and of temptation,
> An age of tears, of envy and of torment,
> A time of languor and of damnation . . .
> *Temps de doleur et de temptacion,*
> *Aages de plour, d'envie et de tourment,*
> *Temps de langour et de dampnacion . . .*

When told that his one-year-old son had died, Philip the Good (1396–1467), Duke of Burgundy, had replied in a tone characteristic of many voices in the pre-modern period, 'If only God had deigned to let me die so young, I would have considered myself fortunate.'

9

But the modern age has not been so liberal – or so kind – with its pessimism.

From the early nineteenth century onwards, Western bookshops have inspired – and unintentionally saddened – their readers with autobiographies of self-made heroes and compendia of advice directed at the not-yet-made, illustrating morality tales of wholesale personal transformation, of the rapid attainment of vast wealth and great happiness.

Benjamin Franklin's *Autobiography* (left incomplete at his death in 1790) was perhaps the originator of the genre, and recounted how a penniless young man, one of seventeen children of a Boston candle-maker, had ended up – entirely through his wits – accruing a fortune and the friendship and respect of the most important people on earth. Franklin's life of self-improvement and the analects he drew from it ('Early to bed, and early to rise, makes a Man healthy, wealthy and wise', 'There are no gains without pains') belonged to a vast literature designed to edify Western nineteenth-century readers. The category included William Mathews's *Getting On in the World* (1874), William Maher's *On the Road to Riches* (1876), Edwin T. Freedley's *The Secret of Success in Life* (1881), Lyman Abbott's *How to Succeed* (1882), William Speer's *The Law of Success* (1885) and Samuel Fallows's *The Problem of Success for Young Men and How to Solve It* (1903).

The trend has not abated. 'Right now you can make a decision,' explained Anthony Robbins (*Awaken the Giant Within*, 1991), 'to go back to school, to master dancing or singing, to take control of your finances, to learn to fly a helicopter ... If you truly decide to, you can do almost anything. So if you don't like the current relationship you're in, make the decision now to change it. If you don't like your current job, change it.'

Robbins offered his own story as evidence of the possibility of change. He had struggled from humble and unhappy circumstances. In his early twenties he had worked as a janitor and had lived in a small, dirty apartment; he had had no girlfriend, he had spent his evenings at home listening to Neil Diamond and had been thirty-eight pounds overweight. Then, one day, he had abruptly decided to revolutionize his life and had discovered a 'power' in his mind to help him do so:

Anthony Robbins, Awaken the Giant Within, 1991

'I used [this power] to take back control of my physical well-being and permanently rid myself of thirty-eight pounds of fat. Through it, I attracted the woman of my dreams, married her and created the family I desired. I used this power to change my income from subsistence level to over one million dollars a year. It moved me from my tiny apartment (where I was washing my dishes in the bathtub because there was no kitchen) to my family's current home, the Del Mar Castle.'

There was no reason not to follow his example, particularly – Robbins noted – if we happened to live in democratic and capitalist societies in which 'we all have the capability to carry out our dreams'.

10

The growth of the mass media has further helped to raise expectations. Alfred Harmsworth, founder of Britain's *Daily Mail,* candidly explained at his newspaper's launch in 1896 that his ideal reader was a man in the street 'worth one hundred pounds per annum' who could be enticed to dream of being 'tomorrow's thousand pound man' – while in America, *Ladies' Home Journal* (launched in 1883), *Cosmopolitan* (1886), *Munsey's* (1889) and *Vogue* (1892) brought an expensive life within the imaginative reach of all. Readers of *fin-de-siècle* American *Vogue*, for example, were told who had been on *Nourmahal,* John Jacob Astor's yacht, after the America's Cup race, what the most fashionable young girls were wearing at boarding school, who threw the best parties in Newport and Southampton and what to serve with caviar at dinner (potato and sour cream).

The opportunity to study the lives of people of higher status and forge a connection with them was also increased by the development of radio, film and television. By the 1930s, Americans were collectively spending 150 million hours per week at the cinema, and almost one billion hours listening to the radio. In 1946 0.02 per cent of American households had televisions, by 2000 the figure stood at 98 per cent.

The new media created longings in its audience not only through its content, but also through the advertisements they carried. Advertising, which had begun in an amateurish way in the United States in the 1830s, was, by 1900, a business worth $500 million a year. In that year, a giant Coca-Cola sign was placed to one side of Niagara Falls, while an advert for Mennen's Toilet Powder was suspended over the gorge.

11

When defenders of modern societies have sought to make a case to sceptics, their task has not been difficult: they have had only to point to the enormous wealth that modern societies are able to generate for their members.

In his *Inquiry into the Nature and Causes of the Wealth of Nations* (1776), Adam Smith sarcastically compared the awe-inspiring productivity of modern societies with the dismal resources open to primitive hunting and gathering ones. Early societies were, in Smith's account, steeped in terrible poverty. Harvests rarely yielded enough food, there was a shortage of basic goods and, in serious crises, children, elderly relatives and the poor were left 'to be devoured by wild beasts'. But, because of their innovative mode of production, described by Smith as 'the division of labour', modern societies could provide for all their members. No one but the romantic and ignorant could therefore wish to live anywhere else: 'A workman, even of the lowest and poorest order, if he is frugal and industrious, may [in a modern society] enjoy a greater share of the necessaries and conveniences of life than it is possible for any savage to acquire.'

12

But twenty-two years earlier, a single, shrill, eccentric but un-settlingly persuasive voice had been heard to argue in favour of an unlikely character: the savage. Was it possible, asked Jean-Jacques Rousseau in his *Discourse on the Origin of Inequality* (1754), that it might in fact be the savage and not – as everyone had grown used to thinking – the modern worker who was the better off of the pair?

Rousseau's argument hung on a thesis about wealth: that wealth does not involve having many things. It involves having what we *long* for. Wealth is not an absolute. It is relative to desire. Every time we seek something we cannot afford, we grow poorer, whatever our resources. And every time we feel satisfied with what we have, we can be counted as rich, however little we may actually own.

There are two ways to make people richer, reasoned Rousseau: to give them more money or to restrain their desires. Modern societies have succeeded spectacularly at the first option but, by continuously inflaming appetites, they have at the same time helped to negate a share of their most impressive achievements. The most effective way to feel wealthy may not be to try to make more money. It may be to distance ourselves – practically and emotionally – from anyone whom we consider to be our equal but who has become richer than ourselves. Rather than trying to become bigger fish, we could concentrate our energies on gathering around us smaller companions next to whom our own size will not trouble us.

In so far as advanced societies provide us with historically elevated incomes, they appear to make us richer. But in truth, the net effect of these societies may be to impoverish us because, by foster-ing unlimited expectations, they keep open a permanent gap between what we want and what we can afford, who we are and who we might be. Such societies may leave us feeling more deprived than primitive savages who, added Rousseau (his argument reaching its more implausible limits), were certain they lacked for nothing in the world if they had a roof over their heads, a few apples and nuts to eat and could spend their evenings playing with 'some crude musical instrument' or 'using sharp-edged stones to make a fishing canoe'.

Rousseau's comparison of the levels of happiness of primitive and modern man returns us to William James's emphasis on the role of expectations in determining levels of happiness. We may be happy with little when we have come to expect little. And we may be miserable with much when we have been taught to expect everything.

Rousseau's naked savages had few possessions. But, unlike their successors in their Taj Mahals, they were at least able to feast on the great wealth that comes from aspiring to very little.

13
The price we have paid for expecting to be so much more than our ancestors is a perpetual anxiety that we are far from being all we might be.

IV.
MERITOCRACY

Three Useful Old Stories about Failure

1

To occupy a low position in the social hierarchy is rarely pleasant from a material point of view, but it is not everywhere and at all times equally psychologically painful. The impact of poverty on self-esteem will to an important extent be decided by the way that poverty is interpreted and accounted for by the community.

While the material progress of the West over two millennia is incontestable, explanations for why one might be poor and what one's value to society might be could be said to have grown notably more punitive and emotionally awkward in the modern era, an evolution contributing a fourth explanation for any anxiety about having or acquiring low status.

2

From approximately AD 30, when Jesus began his ministry, to the latter half of the twentieth century, the lowest in Western societies had to hand three stories about their significance which, while they could be believed, must have worked a profoundly consoling, anxiety-reducing effect on their listeners.

First Story
The Poor are Not Responsible for Their Condition
and are the Most Useful in Society

If one had asked a member of a Western medieval or pre-modern country on what basis society was divided into rich and poor,

A representation of the three Orders of Society, clergy, nobility, peasantry, from the Image du Monde, *French School, 13th century*

peasant and nobleman, the question would most likely have seemed bizarre: God had simply willed the division.

Yet alongside this inflexible belief in a three-class structure – peasantry, clergy and nobility – came an unusually strong appreciation of the way that the different classes depended on each other and hence an unusually strong appreciation of the value of the poorest class. A theory of mutual dependence held that the peasantry was no less vital and hence no less worthy of dignity than the nobility or clergy. The lives of peasants might be hard (unalterably so), but it was known that without them the other two classes would soon founder. It might have seemed ungenerous of John of Salisbury to compare the poor to a pair of feet and the rich to a head, but this otherwise insulting metaphor had the benefit of reminding the wealthy to treat the poor with respect if they wanted to stay alive just as they knew to treat their feet with respect in order to walk.

Patronization was accompanied by its more advantageous twin, paternalism. If the poor were like children, then it was the task of the rich to behave like loving parents. Medieval art and literature were therefore peppered with condescending but generous praise of the peasantry. It wasn't overlooked that Jesus himself had been a carpenter.

In his *Colloquy* (*c.* 1015), Aelfric, the Abbot of Eynsham, argued that by far the most important members of society were the plough-men, for though one might be able to survive without a nobleman or a clergyman, no one could survive without food and therefore peasants. In 1036, Bishop Gerard of Cambrai preached a sermon explaining that, although ploughmen's work was dull and hard, it made all other intellectually more elevated kinds of work possible. Good people hence had to honour peasants. Hans Rosenplüt of Nuremberg was one poet among many who felt moved to write in praise of the 'noble ploughman'. In his poem 'Der Bauern Lob' (*c.* 1450) he intoned that, in all God's creation, no one was as exalted as the peasant:

It is often hard labour for him when he wields the plough
With which he feeds all the world; lords, townsmen, and artisans.
But if there were no peasant, our lives would be in a very sad condition.

A peasant reaping the fields, from a psalter calendar, England, c. 1250–75

Such words may not have softened the earth through which the peasants had to drive their ploughs, but when considered together with the attitude underlying them they must nevertheless have helped to foster in the peasantry a welcome sense of their own dignity.

The Limbourg Brothers, Peasants at Work on a Feudal Estate, 1400-1416

Second Story
Low Status Has No Moral Connotations

There was another useful story at large, this one derived more directly from scripture. From a Christian perspective, neither wealth nor poverty was an accurate guide to moral worth. Jesus was the highest man, the most blessed, and yet on earth he had been poor, ruling out any simple equation between righteousness and worldly position.

In so far as Christianity ever strayed from a neutral view of money, it was to the advantage of the poor, for, in the Christian schema, the source of all goodness was the recognition of one's dependence on God. Anything that encouraged the belief that one might lead a contented life without his grace was evil, and so money was dubious because of the worldly pleasures and the sense of freedom it offered.

But the hardships to which the poor were subject made them turn more naturally to God for assistance. In the soothing stories of the New Testament, the poor therefore witnessed the rich failing to fit through the eyes of needles, they heard that they would inherit the earth and were assured that they would be among the first through the gates of the heavenly kingdom.

Third Story
The Rich are Sinful and Corrupt and Owe their Wealth to their Robbery of the Poor

There was a third story available to soften the blow of poverty and a low social position. According to this narrative, which assumed its greatest influence between approximately 1754 and 1989, the poor were reminded that the rich were thieving and corrupt and had attained their privileges through plunder and deception, rather than virtue and talent. Furthermore, the privileged had so rigged society that the poor could not hope to improve their lot individually, however talented and willing they might be. The only hope for them was mass social protest – and revolution.

It was Jean-Jacques Rousseau who gave the story one of its earliest recitals, arguing that the powerful had, since the dawn of time, assumed and maintained their position by means of robbery: 'The first person who, having enclosed a plot of land, took it into his head to say *this is mine* and found people simple enough to believe him, was the true founder of civil society. What crimes, wars, murders, what miseries and horrors would the human race have been spared, had someone pulled up the stakes or filled in the ditch and cried out to his fellow men: "Do not listen to this impostor. You are lost if you forget that the fruits of the earth belong to all and the earth to no one!"' (*Discourse on the Origin of Inequality*, 1754).

A hundred years later, Karl Marx gave the story its next great lease of life, placing what had in Rousseau's hands been a raw cry of social protest on to an apparently scientific footing. There was, for Marx, an inherently exploitative dynamic within the capitalist system, for every employer tried to hire workers for less money than he or she could make from selling these employees' products and then pocketed the difference as 'profit'. Though such profit was hailed in the capitalist press as the employer's reward for 'risk-taking' and 'enterprise', Marx insisted that these words were mere euphemisms for theft.

He accused the bourgeoisie of being the latest incarnation of a master class that had unjustly held sway over the poor since the beginning of time. However humane the bourgeoisie might seem, their ruthlessness lay just below a civilized surface. In *Capital, Volume I* (1887), Marx addressed the bourgeoisie in the voice of the worker: 'You may be a model citizen, perhaps a member of the Society for the Prevention of Cruelty to Animals, and have the odour of sanctity to boot, but you are a creature with no heart in its breast.' Evidence of this callousness was to be found in any nineteenth-century mill, bakery, dockyard, hotel or office. Workers were diseased, they died young of cancer and respiratory illnesses, their jobs denied them the chance of a proper family life, gave them no time to develop an intellectual understanding of their position and left them anxious and without security: 'For all its stinginess, capitalist production is thoroughly wasteful with human material.' So Marx urged the human material to rise up against its masters and to reclaim what it was rightfully owed. As *The Communist Manifesto* (1848) thundered, 'Let the ruling classes tremble at a Communist revolution. The proletarians have nothing to lose but their chains. They have a world to win. WORKING MEN OF ALL COUNTRIES, UNITE!'

Shortly before the publication of the *Manifesto*, Marx's associate, Friedrich Engels, had travelled to Manchester and described at first hand the suffering of the poor in the new cities of the Industrial Revolution. *The Condition of the Working-class in England* (1845) shared Marx's view of why society was split into classes: the rich were wealthy not because they were clever or energetic or diligent, but because they were cunning and mean. And the poor were poor not because they were idle or drunk or dim, but because they were being blindfolded and abused by their masters. The bourgeoisie depicted in Engels's account took self-interest to sobering extremes: 'It is money gain which alone determines them. I once went into Manchester with a bourgeois, and spoke to him of the bad, unwholesome method of building, the frightful condition of the working-people's quarters, and asserted that I had never seen so ill-built a city. The man listened quietly to the end, and then said at the corner where we parted: "And yet there is a great deal of money made here. Good morning, sir." It is utterly indifferent to the English bourgeois whether his working-men starve or not, if only he makes money. All the conditions of life are measured by money, and what brings no money is nonsense, unpractical, idealistic bosh.'

Life might not have been pleasant in the slums of Manchester in the 1840s, but to hear that the principal reason why one had ended up there was the monstrosity of one's employers and the endemic corruption of the economic system (against which it was vain for the poor ever to try to act singly) would have offered a sustaining sense of moral superiority and dampened any tendencies to feel shame at one's haggard condition.

3

In their different ways, these three stories offered consolation for low status between AD 30 and 1989. They were not, of course, the only stories in circulation, but they had power and were widely listened to. They oriented the less fortunate towards three sustaining ideas: that they were the true wealth creators in society and were therefore worthy of respect; that earthly status had no moral value in the eyes of God; and that the rich were in any case not worth honouring, for they were both unscrupulous and destined to meet a bad end in a set of imminent and just proletarian revolutions.

Three Anxiety-inducing New Stories about Success

1

Unfortunately three other, more troubling, stories began to form around the middle of the eighteenth century and steadily gained in influence, challenging the previous stories in public opinion.

The rise of these stories may have been accompanied by momentous material improvements across society but, at a psychological level, their contribution was to make low status all the harder to endure and all the more worrying to contemplate.

First Story
The Rich are the Useful Ones, Not the Poor

Writing in *c.* 1015, Aelfric, the Abbot of Eynsham, had emphasized that wealth was created almost exclusively by the poor, who rose before dawn, ploughed the fields and collected the harvests. The critical nature of their work gave them a right to the honour of all those above them in the hierarchy. The abbot was not alone in thus crediting ordinary workers. For centuries, economic orthodoxy stated that the wealth-generating classes in society were the working ones. The rich simply dissipated resources through their taste for extravagance and luxury.

This analysis of who could be credited for creating national wealth survived almost unscathed until the spring of 1723, when the London physician Bernard Mandeville published an economic tract in verse, *The Fable of the Bees*, which helped irrevocably to alter the way in which rich and poor were perceived. Mandeville proposed that, contrary to centuries of economic thinking, it was the rich who were in fact the useful ones, because their expenditure provided employment for everyone below them and so helped the weakest in society to survive. Without the rich, the poor would soon be laid out in their graves. Mandeville did not want to suggest that the rich were *nicer* than the poor, in fact, he gleefully pointed out how vain, cruel and fickle they often were. Their desires knew no bounds, they craved applause and failed to understand that happiness did not come through material acquisition. And yet the pursuit and attainment of great wealth were infinitely more useful to society than the patient, unremunerative work of labourers. In judging people's value, one had to look not at their souls (as Christian moralists were inclined to do), but at their effect on others. Judged by this new criterion, there could be no doubt that those who amassed money (in trade, industry or agriculture) and spent much of it (on absurd luxuries; by building unnecessary storehouses or country seats) were more beneficially engaged than the poor. As Mandeville's subtitle to his work put it, it was a case of 'Private Vices, Public Benefits'. 'It is the sensual courtier who sets no limit to his luxury, the fickle strumpet who invents new fashions every week, the profuse rake and the lavish heir [who most effectively help the poor]. He that gives most trouble to thousands of his neighbours and invents the most otiose manufactures is, right or wrong, the greatest friend to society. Mercers, upholsterers, tailors and many others would be starved in half a year's time if *pride* and *luxury* were at once to be banished from the nation.'

Mandeville's thesis shocked his initial audience (as he intended it to), but it went on to convince almost all the great economists and political thinkers of the eighteenth century and beyond. In his essay *Of Luxury* (1752), Hume repeated the Mandevilleian argument in favour of the pursuit of riches and of expenditure on superfluous goods on the grounds that this, rather than the work of the poor, was what created wealth: 'In a nation where there is no demand for superfluities, men sink into indolence, lose all enjoyment of life, and are useless to the public, which cannot maintain or support its fleets and armies.'

Twenty-four years later, Hume's countryman Adam Smith deepened the theory further in *The Wealth of Nations* (1776), perhaps the most beguiling defence of the utility of the rich ever written. Smith began by admitting that great sums of money did not always bring happiness: 'Riches leave a man always as much and sometimes more exposed than before to anxiety, to fear and to sorrow.' He commented sarcastically on those foolish enough to devote their entire lives to chasing 'baubles and trinkets'. But at the same time he expressed immense gratitude that such creatures abounded. The whole of civilization, and the welfare of all societies, depended on people's desire and ability to accumulate unnecessary capital and show off their wealth. It was this 'which first prompted men to cultivate the ground, to build houses, to found cities and commonwealths and to invent all the sciences and arts which ennoble and embellish human life; which have entirely changed the whole face of the globe, have turned the rude forests of nature into agreeable and fertile plains, and made the trackless and barren ocean a new fund of subsistence'.

In economic theories of old, the rich had been condemned for taking too large a share of what was thought to be a finite pool of national wealth. Smith acknowledged that it was tempting to view a man of 'huge estate' as a 'pest to society, as a monster, a great fish who devours up all the lesser ones'. But this was to forget that there was no finite pool of wealth, the pool could always be expanded through the efforts and ambitions of entrepreneurs and traders. The great fish, far from devouring the lesser ones, in practice helped them, by spending money and providing them with employment. The great fish might be arrogant and coarse, but their vices were, through the operations of the market place, transformed into virtues – as Smith explained in possibly the most famous passage of capitalist economics: 'In spite of their natural selfishness and rapacity, though they mean only their own convenience, though the sole end which they propose from the labours of all the thousands whom they employ be the gratification of their own vain and insatiable desires, the rich divide with the poor the produce of all their improvements. They are led by an invisible hand to make nearly the same distribution of the necessities of life, which would have been made, had the earth been divided into equal portions among all its inhabitants, and thus, without intending it, without knowing it, advance the interest of society, and afford means to the multiplication of the species.'

In societies where wealthy people were given sufficient opportunities to trade and develop industry, 'so great a quantity of everything is produced', wrote Smith, 'that there is enough both to gratify the slothful and oppressive profusions of the great and at the same time abundantly to supply the wants of the artisan and peasant'.

Here was an unexpectedly delightful story for the better off. From having been the villains of economic theory since the early days of Christianity, they now found themselves redescribed as heroes. It was the rich who deserved the honour for helping all social classes below them. It was they who housed the poor and fed the needy, and they who provided for the little fish swimming in their wake. Furthermore, they did this even when they were personally unpleasant; the greedier they were, the better.

The story was less flattering to the poor; while the rich were the creators of national prosperity, they were allotted a meek, functional role and might even be accused of draining resources through their excessive numbers and reliance on welfare and charity. Already burdened by material deprivation, the new economic story added to their lot the implicit condemnation of many in the comfortably off classes. It now seemed rather less fitting for poets to devote their verses to celebrating the nobility of ploughmen.

Second Story
One's Status Does have Moral Connotations

Central to traditional Christian thought was the claim that one's status carried no moral connotations. Jesus had been the highest man, but he had been a carpenter. Pilate had been an important imperial official, but a sinner. It therefore made no sense to believe that one's place in the social hierarchy reflected actual qualities. One could be intelligent, kind, resourceful, quick and creative and be sweeping floors. And one might be chinless, degenerate, *fin de race*, sadistic and foolish and be governing the nation.

The claim of a disjuncture between rank and value was hard to contest when, for centuries, positions were distributed according to bloodlines and family connections rather than talent and when, as a result, Western societies were filled with kings who couldn't govern, lords who couldn't manage their estates, commanders who didn't understand the principles of battle, peasants who were brighter than their masters and maids who knew more than their mistresses.

The situation remained unchanged until the middle of the eighteenth century, when the first voices began to question the hereditary principle. Was it really wise to hand down a business to a son irrespective of his intelligence? Were the children of royalty always best fitted to run countries? To highlight the follies of the principle, comparisons were made with an area of life where a meritocratic system had long been entrenched and accepted by even committed supporters of hereditary privilege: the literary world. When it came to choosing a book, what mattered was whether it was good rather than whether the author's parents had been literary or wealthy. A talented father did not guarantee success, or an ignominious one failure. Why, then, not import this method of judgement into appointments in political or economic life?

'I smile to myself when I contemplate the ridiculous insignificance into which literature and all the sciences would sink, were they made hereditary', commented Thomas Paine in *The Rights of Man* (1791), 'and I carry the same idea into governments. A hereditary governor is as inconsistent as a hereditary author. I know not whether Homer or Euclid had sons; but I will venture an opinion that if they had, and had left their works unfinished, those sons could not have completed them.'

Napoleon shared Paine's stance and, early on in his rule, was the first Western leader openly to begin instituting what he was to term a system of *'carrières ouvertes aux talents'*, 'careers open to talent'. 'I made most of my generals *de la boue*,' he proudly remarked on St Helena at the end of his life. 'Whenever I found talent, I rewarded it.' There was substance to the boast. Napoleonic France witnessed the abolition of feudal privileges and the institution of the Legion of Honour, the first title open to people from every social rank. The education system was reformed: *lycées* were opened to all and a poly-technic started in 1794, which offered generous state subsidies for poorer pupils (in the polytechnic's early years, half the students were the sons of peasants and artisans). Many of Napoleon's leading offi-cials were from modest backgrounds: his prefects at the Ministry of the Interior, his scientific advisers and senators. In Napoleon's words, hereditary nobles were 'the curse of the nation, imbeciles and hereditary asses!'

Even after his fall, Napoleon's ideas endured and won over influ-ential minds in Europe and the United States. Ralph Waldo Emerson wished to see 'every man placed where he belongs, with so much power confided to him as he would carry and use'. Thomas Carlyle expressed indignation at the way the children of the rich squandered their money, while those of the poor were denied an education: 'What shall we say of the Idle Aristocracy, the owners of the soil of England; whose recognised function is that of handsomely consum-ing the rents of England and shooting the partridges of England?' He inveighed against those who had never done anything, benefited any-one, who had not had to prove themselves in any field and had been handed their privileges on a plate. He imagined the typical English aristocrat: 'luxuriously housed up, screened from all work, from want, danger, hardship. He sits serene, amid appliances, and has his work done by other men. And such a man calls himself a *noble*-man? His fathers worked for him, he says; or successfully gambled for him. It is the law of the land, and is thought to be the law of the Universe that this man shall have no task laid on him except that of eating his cooked victuals and not flinging himself out of the window!'

Like many nineteenth-century reformers, what Carlyle wanted was not a world in which everyone was financially equal, but one in which both the elite and the poor would merit their inequalities. 'Europe requires a real aristocracy,' he wrote, 'only it must be an aristocracy of talent. False aristocracies are insupportable.' What Carlyle wanted – though the word had not yet been coined – was a meritocracy.

The new ideology of meritocracy competed with two alternative notions of social organization: the egalitarian principle, with its call for complete equality in the distribution of goods between humans; and the hereditary principle, with its belief that titles and posts (and partridge shoots) should be automatically transferred to the children of the wealthy. Like aristocrats of old, meritocrats were prepared to accept a great deal of inequality but, like radical egalitarians, they wanted an initial period of complete equality of opportunity. If everyone had had the same education and the same chance to gain access to careers, differences in income and prestige would then be justified by reference to individuals' own talents and weaknesses; consequently there would be no need to equalize incomes. Privileges would be merited – as would hardships.

Social legislation in the nineteenth and twentieth centuries saw the triumph of the meritocratic principle. Equal opportunities were, at varying speeds and with different degrees of sincerity, promoted by the governments of every Western country. It came to be generally accepted that a decent secondary and, in many cases, university education should be made available to all citizens irrespective of income. The United States led the way in 1824 with the opening of the first truly publicly supported high school. By the time of the Civil War there were three hundred such high schools; by 1890 there were two thousand five hundred. In the 1920s, it was the turn of university education to be reformed along meritocratic lines through the development of the SAT (Scholastic Assessment Test) system. Its founders, the president of Harvard University, James Conant, and the head of the government's Educational Testing Service, Henry Chauncey, aimed to develop a scientifically proven meritocratic test which could assess the intelligence of all students fairly and dispassionately, thereby ending old-school bias, racism and snobbery in university admissions. Rather than being judged by who their fathers were or how they dressed, American pupils would now be ranked according to their real worth – which, according to Conant and Chauncey's understanding of the term, meant their ability to solve problems like:

Pick out the antonyms from among these four words:
    obdurate   spurious   ductile   recondite

And:

Say which word, or both or neither, has the same meaning as the first word:
        impregnable   terile   vacuous
        nominal   exorbitant   didactic

Those who succeeded in such challenges would merit their success, their ensuing membership of country clubs and their jobs in Wall Street firms. In the words of Conant, the SAT was: 'A new type of social instrument whose proper use may be the means of salvation of the classlessness of the nation ... a means of recapturing social flexibility, a means of approximating more nearly the American ideal.'

This American ideal did not, of course, involve equality, merely an initial period of strictly policed equal opportunity. If everyone had had the same chance to go to school and enter university and to find the antonym among a list of words, then there would be justice in any aristocracy that subsequently emerged among Americans.

By 1948, the year of the publication of the Universal Declaration of Human Rights, its twenty-sixth provision had become, in many parts of Europe and the United States at least, more or less a reality: 'Everyone has the right to education. Education shall be free, certainly in the elementary and fundamental stages. Elementary education shall be compulsory. Technical and professional education shall be made generally available and higher education shall be equally accessible to all on the basis of merit.'

Alongside these educational reforms came legislation promoting equal opportunities in the workplace. In Britain the landmark meritocratic measure was the opening of the civil service to competitive examinations in 1870. For centuries the service had been home to the penniless and dim-witted relatives of aristocrats, with some catastrophic results for the empire. By the middle of the nineteenth century, the costs of employing these well-mannered, partridge-shooting fools had grown so high that two government officials, Sir Stafford Northcote and Sir Charles Trevelyan, were asked to consider an alternative system of recruitment. Having studied the civil service for a few months, Trevelyan explained in a letter to *The Times*, 'There can be no doubt that our high aristocracy have been accustomed to employ the service as a means of providing for the waifs and strays of their families – as a sort of foundling hospital where those who had no energy to make their way in open professions might receive a nominal office for life at the expense of the public.'

Seventy years later, in *The Lion and the Unicorn* (1941), George Orwell was still protesting against the evils of nepotism. Britain needed a revolution, he said, but one without 'red flags and street fighting'; instead, it had to involve 'a fundamental shift of power' towards those who deserved it: 'What is wanted is a conscious open revolt by ordinary people against inefficiency, class privilege and the rule of the old. Right through our national life we have got to fight against privilege, against the notion that a half-witted public-schoolboy is better for command than an intelligent mechanic. Although there are gifted and honest *individuals* among them, we have got to break the grip of the moneyed class as a whole. England has got to assume its real shape.'

Throughout the developed world, replacing halfwits with the meritorious became the leading ambition behind employment reform. In the United States equality of opportunity was pursued with particular intensity. In March 1961, less than two months after assuming office, President John F. Kennedy established a Committee on Equal Opportunity, charged with ending employment discrimination in all its forms in government departments and private businesses. A stream of legislation followed: the Equal Pay Act (1963), the Civil Rights Act (1964), the Equal Employment Opportunity Act (1964), the Older Americans Act (1965), the Age Discrimination in Employment Act (1967), the Equal Credit Opportunity Act (1976) and the Americans with Disabilities Act (1990). With such legislation in place, however old one happened to be and whatever one's age, colour or sex, it was plausible to believe that one would be guaranteed a fair opportunity to succeed.

Though progress towards a thoroughly meritocratic system may have been slow, at times haphazard and as yet incomplete, from the middle of the nineteenth century, especially in the United States and Britain, it began to influence public perceptions of the relative virtues of the poor and the wealthy. If jobs and rewards were being handed out after a dispassionate interview and examination, then it was no longer possible to argue that worldly position was wholly divorced from inner qualities, as many Christian thinkers had proposed, or to claim that the wealthy and powerful must necessarily have attained their positions through corrupt means, as Rousseau and Marx had suggested. Once the partridge-shooters had been ejected from the civil service and replaced with the intelligent offspring of the working classes, once SAT examinations had emptied Ivy League universities of the witless sons and daughters of East Coast plutocrats and filled them with the hard-working children of shop-owners instead, it became harder to argue that status was earned entirely as the result of a rigged system.

An increasing faith in a reliable connection between merit and worldly position in turn endowed money with a new moral quality. When wealth had been handed down the generations according to bloodlines and connections, it was natural to dismiss the idea that money was any indicator of virtue besides that of having been born to the right parents. But in a meritocratic world, where prestigious and well-paid jobs could be secured only on the basis of one's own intelligence and ability, it now seemed that wealth might be a sound sign of character. The rich were not only wealthier; they might also be plain *better*.

Over the nineteenth century, many Christian thinkers, especially in the United States, changed their views of money accordingly. American Protestant denominations suggested that God required his followers to lead a life that was successful both temporally and spiritually; fortunes in this world were evidence that one deserved a good place in the next – an attitude reflected in the Reverend Thomas P. Hunt's bestseller of 1836, *The Book of Wealth: In Which it is Proved from the Bible that it is the Duty of Every Man to Become Rich.* Wealth came to be described as a reward from God for holiness. John D. Rockefeller was unabashed to state that it was the Lord who had made him rich, while William Lawrence, the Episcopal Bishop of Massachusetts, writing in 1892, argued: 'In the long run, it is only to the man of morality that wealth comes. We, like the Psalmist, occasionally see the wicked prosper, but only occasionally. Godliness is in league with riches.'

Thanks to the meritocratic ideal, multitudes were granted the opportunity to fulfil themselves. Gifted and intelligent individuals, who for centuries had been held down within an immobile, caste-like hierarchy, were now free to express their talents on a more or less level playing field. No longer were background, gender, race or age impassable obstacle to advancement. An element of justice had finally entered into the distribution of rewards.

But there was, inevitably, a darker side to the story for those of low status. If the successful merited their success, it necessarily followed that the failures had to merit their failure. In a meritocratic age, justice appeared to enter into the distribution of poverty as well as wealth. Low status came to seem not merely regrettable, but also *deserved.*

To succeed financially without inheritance or advantages in an economic meritocracy lent individuals an element of personal vali-dation that the nobleman of old, who had been given his money and his castle by his father, had never been able to experience. But, at the same time, financial failure became associated with a sense of shame that the peasant of old, denied all chances in life, had also thankful-ly been spared.

The question why, if one was in any way good, clever or able, one was still poor became more acute and painful for the unsuccessful to have to answer (to themselves and others) in a new meritocratic age.

Third Story
The Poor are Sinful and Corrupt
and Owe their Poverty to their Stupidity ·

There turned out to be no shortage of people willing to answer the question on behalf of the poor during the nineteenth and twentieth centuries. For a certain vocal constituency, it was clear (and scientifically provable) that the poor owed their position to their own stupidity and degeneracy.

With the rise of an economic meritocracy the poor moved, in certain quarters, from being described as 'unfortunate', the target of the charity and guilt of the rich, to being described as 'failures', fair targets of contempt in the eyes of robust self-made individuals, who were disinclined to feel ashamed about their mansions or shed crocodile tears for those whose company they had escaped.

There could have been no more telling expression of the idea of satisfactory justice behind the distribution of wealth and poverty than the nineteenth-century philosophy of Social Darwinism. Social Darwinists proposed that all humans began by facing a fair struggle over scarce resources: money, jobs, esteem. Some gained the upper hand in this contest, not because of improper advantages or luck but because they were intrinsically better than those they outpaced. The rich were not better from a moral point of view. They were, intimidatingly, naturally better. They were more potent, their seed was stronger, their minds were cannier, they were the tigers of the human jungle predestined by biology – a new, godlike concept before which the nineteenth century genuflected – to triumph over others. Biology wanted the rich to be rich and the poor to be poor.

Furthermore, Social Darwinists insisted that the sufferings and early deaths of the poor were beneficial to society as a whole, and should therefore not be prevented by government interference. The weak were nature's mistakes and had to be allowed to perish before they could reproduce and thereby contaminate the rest of the population. Just as the animal kingdom threw up its share of malformed creatures, so too did the human world. The kindest thing one could do was to let the downtrodden die without charity.

In his *Social Statics* (1851) the English Social Darwinist Herbert Spencer argued that biology itself disagreed with the concept of charity: 'It seems hard that widows and orphans should be left to struggle for life or death. Nevertheless, when regarded not separately, but in connection with the interests of universal humanity, these harsh fatalities are seen to be full of beneficence – the same beneficence which brings to early graves the children of diseased parents ... Under the natural order of things society is constantly excreting its unhealthy, imbecile, slow, vacillating, faithless members. If they are sufficiently complete to live, they do live, and it is well that they should live. If they are not sufficiently complete to live, they die, and it is best they should die.'

Spencer's doctrines found a receptive audience among the self-made plutocrats who dominated American business and the media. Social Darwinism provided them with an apparently impregnable scientific argument to rebut what many of them were already suspicious of, and what harmed them at an economic level: trade unions, Marxism and socialism. In a triumphant tour of America in 1882, Spencer addressed gatherings of business leaders, flattering them by comparing them to the alpha beasts of the human jungle and sparing them any need for charity or guilt towards their weaker brethren.

Even many who did not directly subscribe to a Social Darwinist perspective shared one of the philosophy's key assumptions: that it was unnecessary and possibly wrong to offer welfare to the poor. If everyone had the power to become successful by their own efforts, then political action to assist the lower classes only rewarded failure.

In his *Self-help* (1859), the Scottish doctor Samuel Smiles, after encouraging deprived young people to set themselves high goals, educate themselves and spend money carefully, railed against any government that might help them along this path: 'Whatever is done *for* men takes away from them the stimulus and necessity of doing things for themselves. The value of legislation as an agent in human advancement has been much over-estimated. No laws, however stringent, can ever make the idle industrious, the thriftless provident or the drunken sober.'

The Scottish-American magnate Andrew Carnegie, despite his philanthropy, at heart held a similarly pessimistic view of the uses of welfare: 'Of every thousand dollars spent in so-called charity nine hundred and fifty of them had better be thrown into the sea,' he remarked in his *Autobiography* (1920). 'Every drunken vagabond or lazy idler supported by alms is a source of moral infection to a neighbourhood. It will not do to teach the hard-working, industrious man that there is an easier path by which his wants can be supplied. The less emotion the better. Neither the individual nor the race is improved by alms-giving. Those worthy of assistance, except in rare cases, seldom require assistance. The really valuable men of the race never do.'

In the harsher climate of opinion that gestated in the fertile corners of meritocratic societies, it became possible to argue that the social hierarchy rigorously reflected the qualities of the members on every rung of the ladder and so thus conditions were already in place for good people to succeed and the drones to flounder – attenuating the need for charity, welfare, redistributive measures or simple compassion.

Andrew Carnegie, self-made industrialist,
the wealthiest man in the world, 1835–1919

2

Michael Young, *The Rise of the Meritocracy* (London, 1958):
'Today all persons, however humble, know they have had every chance ... If they have been labelled "dunce" repeatedly they cannot any longer pretend ... Are they not bound to recognize that they have an inferior status, not as in the past because they were denied opportunity, but because they *are* inferior?'

3

To the injury of poverty, a meritocratic system now added the insult of shame.

V.
DEPENDENCE

Factors of Dependence

1

In traditional societies, high status may have been inordinately hard to acquire, but it was also pleasantly hard to lose. It was as difficult to stop being a lord as, more darkly, it was to stop being a labourer. What mattered was one's identity at birth, rather than anything one might achieve in one's lifetime through the exercise of one's faculties. What mattered was who one was, seldom what one did.

The great ambition of modern societies has been to institute a comprehensive reversal of the equation, to strip away both inherited privilege and inherited under-privilege in order to make rank dependent on individual achievement – which has primarily come to mean financial achievement. Status now rarely depends on an unchangeable identity handed down the generations, it hangs on one's performance within a fast-moving and implacable economy.

Because of the nature of this economy, the most evident feature of the struggle to achieve status is uncertainty. We contemplate the future in the knowledge that we may be thwarted by colleagues or competitors, we may find we lack the talents to fulfil our chosen goals or we may steer into an inauspicious current in the swells of the market place – any failure being compounded by the possible success of peers.

Anxiety is the handmaiden of contemporary ambition because livelihoods and esteem depend on at least five unpredictable elements, five reasons not to count on either attaining or holding on to a desired position within the hierarchy.

1. Dependence on Fickle Talent

If our status depends on our achievements, then what is generally needed to succeed is talent and – when peace of mind is a priority – reliable control over it. But in most activities, talent is impossible to direct as we please. It can make an appearance for a time, and then unapologetically vanish, leaving careers in pieces. We cannot call the best of ourselves to the fore at will. So far are we from owning the talent we on occasion display, that many of our achievements can seem like the result of gifts from an external agency upon whose erratic arrival or disappearance the course of our lives and our ability to pay for the objects around us depend.

It was the ancient Greeks who found the most acute image to evoke our distressingly volatile relationship with talent in the idea of a Muse. According to Greek mythology, there were nine Muses, each of whom controlled and fitfully bestowed a particular gift. There were Muses for epic poetry, history, love poetry, music, tragedy, hymns, dancing, comedy and astronomy. Victors in any of these fields were careful to remember that their gifts were never truly their own and might be spirited away again at a stroke if the thin-skinned deities changed their minds.

The areas in which Greek Muses were said to operate hardly reflect contemporary concerns. And yet the mythological concept continues to capture something valuable about the weak hold we have upon our powers to achieve – and the subservient, anxious position we are therefore forced to adopt in relation to our futures.

2. Dependence on Luck

Our status also depends on a range of favourable conditions that could loosely be captured by the word 'luck'. It can be luck that places us in the right occupation, with the right skills, at the right time –

and little more than bad luck that denies us the self-same advantages.

But to cite luck as an explanation for the outcome of our lives has, regrettably, grown effectively unacceptable. In less technologically sophisticated eras, when men respected the power of the gods and the unpredictable moods of nature, the idea of one's own and others' lack of control over events had wide currency. Gratitude and blame were routinely placed at the door of external agencies: reference was made to the role of demons, goblins, spirits and gods. Throughout the story of *Beowulf* (*c.* AD 1100), for example, we hear that the success of man depends on the will of the Christian God; describing his defeat of Grendel's mother, Beowulf asserts that 'The fight would have ended straightaway if God had not guarded me.'

But as man's power to control and predict the behaviour of his environment has developed, so the concept of luck or of guardian deities has lost its potency. While it is granted that luck maintains a theoretical role in shaping the course of careers, the evaluation of people proceeds, in practical terms, as if they could fairly be held responsible for their biographies. It would seem unduly (and even suspiciously) modest to ascribe a victory to 'good luck' and, more importantly in this context, pitiable to blame defeat on the opposite. Winners make their own luck, insists the modern mantra, which would have puzzled the ancient Roman worshippers of the Goddess of Fortune or the faithful heroes of *Beowulf*.

It is alarming enough to have to depend for our status on contingent elements. It is harder yet to live in a world so imbued with notions of rational control that it has largely dismissed 'bad luck' as a credible explanation for defeat.

3. Dependence on an Employer

The unpredictability of our condition is further aggravated by the likelihood that we will have to depend for our status on the priorities of an employer.

In the United States in 1907, a book entitled *Three Acres and Liberty* seized the imagination of the reading public. The author, Bolton Hall, began by taking for granted the awkwardness of having to work for someone else, and so told readers that they could regain their freedom by leaving their offices and factories and buying three acres of farmland in middle-America at a reasonable cost. These acres would soon enable them to grow enough food to feed a family of four and to furnish a simple but comfortable home, freeing them of the need to flatter and negotiate with colleagues and superiors. The book was given over to detailed descriptions of how to plant vegetables, make a greenhouse, arrange an orchard and buy livestock (one cow was sufficient for milk and cheese, specified Hall, while ducks were more nutritious than chickens). *Three Acres and Liberty* delivered a message heard with increasing frequency in European and American thought after the middle of the nineteenth century: that to lead a happy life, one should attempt to escape reliance on employers in order to work directly for oneself, at one's own pace, for one's own happiness.

If the message grew more frequent from this period onwards, it was because for the first time a majority of people were ceasing to work on their own farms or in small family businesses and were starting to sell their intelligence and their strength in return for a wage given to them by someone else. In 1800, 20 per cent of the American workforce was employed by another person; by 1900, the figure was 50 per cent; by 2000, 90 per cent. Employers were also taking on more people. In 1800, less than 1 per cent of the American workforce was employed in an organization with 500 or more employees; by 2000, the figure was 55 per cent.

In England, the transition from a nation of small agricultural producers to one of wage earners was accelerated by a scarcity of commonly owned land, which had in the past enabled a portion of the population to survive by growing food for themselves and letting their animals, a cow or a goose, roam free. From the eighteenth century onwards, the majority of 'open' English fields were enclosed behind walls and hedges by powerful landowners. Between 1724 and 1815 around one and a half million acres of land were closed off. In the traditional Marxist analysis (heavily challenged by historians but revealing nonetheless), the enclosure movement heralded the birth of a modern industrial proletariat, defined as a group of people unable to live on their own resources who hence have no option but to sell themselves to an employer at a rate and with conditions sharply weighted in the employer's favour.

The travails of being an employee include not only uncertainty about the duration of one's employment, but also the humiliation of many working practices and dynamics. With most businesses shaped like pyramids, in which a wide base of employees gives way to a narrow tip of managers, the question of who will be rewarded – and who left behind – typically develops into one of the most oppressive of the workplace, and one which, like all anxieties, feeds off uncertainty. Because achievement in most fields is difficult to monitor reliably, the path to promotion or its opposite can acquire an apparently haphazard connection to results. The successful alpinists of organizational pyramids may not be the best at their jobs, but those who have best mastered a range of dark political arts in which civilized life does not usually offer instruction.

Whatever the surface differences between modern businesses and royal courts, perhaps the most penetrating advice on the requirements for survival in the former was written by a number of clear-eyed noblemen with experience of living in the latter in France and Italy between the fifteenth and seventeenth centuries. In retirement, these men collected their thoughts into a series of cynical works written in a tart aphoristic style which continue to push the boundaries of what we would like to believe about others. The offerings of Machiavelli (1469–1527), Guicciardini (1483–1540), La Rochefoucauld (1613–80) and La Bruyère (1645–96) give us an indication of the manoeuvres that workers may, aside from their regular advertised roles, have to perform in order to flourish:

The need to beware of colleagues:
'Men are so false, so insidious, so deceitful and cunning in their wiles, so avid in their own interest, and so oblivious to others' interests, that you cannot go wrong if you believe little and trust less.'

GUICCIARDINI

'We must live with our enemies as if they might one day become our friends, and live with our friends as if they might some time or other become our enemies'.

LA BRUYÈRE

The need to lie and exaggerate:
'The world more often rewards signs of merit than merit itself.'

LA ROCHEFOUCAULD

'If you are involved in important affairs, you must always hide failures and exaggerate successes. It is swindling but since your fate more often depends upon the opinion of others rather than on facts, it is a good idea to create the impression that things are going well.'

GUICCIARDINI

'You are an honest man, and do not make it your business either to please or displease the favourites. You are merely attached to your master and to your duty. You are finished.'

LA BRUYÈRE

The need to threaten:
'It is much safer to be feared than loved. Love is sustained by a bond of gratitude which, because men are excessively self-interested, is broken whenever they see a chance to benefit themselves. But fear is sustained by a dread of punishment that is always effective.'

MACHIAVELLI

'Since the majority of men are either not very good or not very wise, one must rely more on severity than on kindness.' GUICCIARDINI

It may of course be possible to acquire the velvet gloves and iron fists of a courtier and to learn to navigate around colleagues as we might around a reef-ringed coastline – but the need to do so is scarcely calming. From the perspective of an office or factory floor, it is easy to fathom the lure of three acres, half a dozen ducks and liberty.

4. Dependence on an Employer's Profitability

The reliability of one's employment depends not only on the politics within organizations, but also on the ability of companies to remain profitable in market places where producers are rarely able to defend their competitive positions or pricing power for long. If the ferocity of the competition leaves many workforces with anxieties perhaps not dissimilar to those one might have standing on a floe of melting ice, it is because the most effective and rapid way for companies to improve profitability is almost invariably to decimate staffing levels.

Companies under financial pressure will find it hard to resist disposing of workers in countries with high wages in order to hire replacements in faraway lands with low ones. They may also be tempted to improve their profitability by merging with competitors, removing large swathes of a duplicate workforce in the process. Or they may develop robots with which to replace their staff. The Automatic Teller Machine (ATM) was developed in 1968 and first installed the following year in a hole in the wall in a branch of Manhattan's Chemical Bank. Ten years later, there were 50,000 ATMs in the world; by 2000, a million. However technologically impressive, ATMs offered bank tellers few grounds for celebration. One ATM could do the job of no fewer than 37 bank tellers (and rarely fell ill) – as figures soon showed. In the United States, 500,000 people, around half of the workforce in retail banking, lost their jobs between 1980 and 1995, in part because of the invention of these silkily efficient machines.

Employees must in addition worry about the consequences of the pressure on companies to introduce new and better products to the market place. For long stretches of history, the life cycles of goods and services were longer than those of the human beings who produced and consumed them. In Japan, the kimono and *jinbaori* went unchanged for 400 years. In China, people were wearing in the eighteenth century exactly what their ancestors had worn in the sixteenth. Between 1300 and 1660, the design of ploughs did not alter across northern Europe – a stability that must have given artisans and workers a reassuring sense that their businesses would outlive them. But product life cycles have sharply accelerated since the middle of the nineteenth century – destroying workers' confidence in the long-term integrity of their careers.

Rapid defeats at the hands of new products and services are to be found in almost every area of the economy: canals after the invention of the railway, passenger liners after the introduction of the jet engine, horses after the development of the car, typewriters after the birth of the personal computer.

The market's passion for change has a propensity to involve companies in product development costs so high that their very survival can depend on the successful launch of a single item. Companies can resemble palpitating gamblers who, instead of being allowed to retreat cautiously after a good run, are continually forced at gunpoint to risk their assets and the livelihoods of their employees on the outcome of a few wagers or even a single bet, as a result either amassing vast but precarious riches or self-destructing.

5. Dependence on the Global Economy

The survival of companies and their employees is further threatened by the performance of the economy as a whole.

The history of the economies of Western nations has, since the early nineteenth century, been one of repeated cycles of growth and recession. Typically, four or five years of expansion have been followed by one or two years of retraction, with occasional massive retrenchments lasting five or six years. Graphs of national wealth resemble the profiles of angular mountain ranges. Behind all the dips of the graph lie the bankruptcies of long-established firms, the lay-offs of workforces, the closures of factories, the destruction of stock. It may be tempting to attribute these events to unnatural and perhaps even one day avoidable dimensions of economic life. But, despite the efforts of governments and central banks, there seems little that is preventable about such turbulence.

Every cycle is marked by similar themes. It begins when growth picks up and companies invest in new capacity to meet perceived future needs. Production costs tend to rise as do asset prices, especially equities and property, in part driven forward by speculators. The cost of credit is low at this point, which encourages businesses to commit to large capital-intensive factories and offices. But while demand and current output begin to slow, rates of consumption continue to rise. With savings low, personal and commercial borrowing also expand. To satisfy domestic demand, imports rise and exports fall, triggering a balance of payments deficit. The economy is now out of kilter: over-investing, over-consuming, over-borrowing and over-lending. From here, a slide into recession begins. Prices increase because of a combination of the use of less efficient productive capacity, and the growth in the money supply and of speculation. Tight and expensive credit increases the cost of outstanding debt. Asset prices, over-valued in the upswing, fall in value. Borrowers cannot meet payments and the collateral for loans is reduced. Incomes, investment and consumption fall. Companies and entrepreneurs are in distress or go bankrupt; unemployment rises. As confidence evaporates, borrowing and spending continue to fall. Long-term investments made in the previous upswing come on line, which increases supply while depressing prices just as demand is slackening. Companies and households are forced to sell assets at reduced costs, deepening the crisis. Potential buyers wait for the bottom of the market before purchasing, further delaying recovery.

Rather than a sign of hysteria, steady anxiety may seem a plausible response to the real threats of the economic environment.

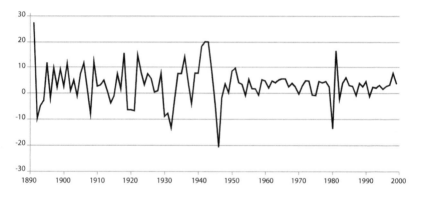

Percentage change in US gross domestic product per capita, 1890–2000

2

If we are anguished by the thought of failure, it is because success offers the only reliable incentive for the world to grant us its good-will. A family bond, a friendship or a sexual attraction may at times render material incentives unnecessary, but it would take a reckless optimist to rely on these currencies for the regular fulfilment of his or her needs. Humans rarely smile without being tempted by robust reasons to do so.

3

Adam Smith, *The Wealth of Nations* (Edinburgh, 1776):

'Man has almost constant occasion for the help of his brethren. [However], it is in vain for him to expect this from their benevolence only. He will be more likely to prevail if he can interest their self-love … It is not from the benevolence of the butcher, the brewer or the baker that we expect our dinner, but from their regard to their own interest. We address ourselves not to their humanity, but to their self-love.'

4

According to one thesis, butchers, brewers and bakers were not always so ruthless. They might once have put victuals on the table not because one was able to offer payment in return, but because one had a pleasant manner or was a distant acquaintance of a relative. Financial self-interest did not, this thesis suggests, always enjoy exclusive rule; it was a recent historical development, a product of the modern age and of advanced capitalism. In the feudal age, this thesis goes on, financial self-interest was strongly counterbalanced by non-material considerations. Workers were held to be members of their employers' extended families and were shown a degree of loyalty and gratitude. Christian teachings helped to foster an atmosphere of concern for the vulnerable and hungry – and a tacit agreement that, in difficult conditions, they would be cared for.

But these patriarchal, communal relationships were, this self-same thesis alleges, destroyed by the bourgeoisie's ascent to power in the second half of the eighteenth century. The bourgeois class, hugely powerful through its command of capital and technology, was interested only in wealth. Unsentimental and utilitarian, it viewed employees as means to its acquisitive ends, it cared nothing for their families, it would not be dictated to by the needs of the sick, the old and the wide-eyed young. At the same time, populations gravitated to large cities, where neighbourly care was destroyed by a competitive, hurried atmosphere. To add to the woes of the vulnerable, Christianity lost its grip on the imagination of those holding the levers of power, and respect for the poor and feelings of community dissipated along with it.

In *The Communist Manifesto* (1848), Karl Marx, the most forceful proponent of this thesis, described the triumph of financial concerns in visionary, apocalyptic prose: 'The bourgeoisie has ... pitilessly torn asunder the motley feudal ties that bound man to his "natural superiors" and has left remaining no other nexus between man and man than naked self-interest, than callous "cash payment". It has drowned the most heavenly ecstasies of religious fervour, of chivalrous enthusiasm, of philistine sentimentalism, in the icy water of egotistical calculation. It has resolved personal worth into exchange value.'

In his *Groundwork of the Metaphysic of Morals* (1785), Immanuel Kant had argued that behaving morally towards other people required that one respect them 'for themselves' instead of using them as a 'means' for one's enrichment or glory. With reference to Kant, Marx now accused the bourgeoisie, and its new science, economics, of practising 'immorality' on a grand scale: '[Economics] knows the worker only as a working animal – as a beast reduced to strictest bodily needs.' The wages paid to employees were, said Marx, just 'like the oil which is applied to wheels to keep them turning. The true purpose of work is no longer man, but money.'

5

Marx may have been a poor historian, erratically idealizing the pre-industrial past and unduly castigating the bourgeoisie, but his theories retain a value in capturing and dramatizing an inescapable degree of conflict between employer and employee.

Beneath many regional variations and differences in style and management, the rationale of almost any commercial organization can be broken down into a simple and arid equation:

INPUT OUTPUT

Raw Materials + Labour + Machinery = Product + Profit

Every organization will attempt to gather raw materials, labour and machinery at the lowest possible price to combine them into a product that can be sold at the highest possible price. From the economic perspective, there are no differences between any of the elements in the input side of the equation. All are commodities which the rational organization will seek to source cheaply and handle efficiently in the search for profit.

And yet, troublingly, there is one difference between 'labour' and other elements which conventional economics does not have a means to represent, or give weight to, but which is nevertheless unavoidably present in the world: the fact that labour feels pain.

When production lines grow prohibitively expensive, these may be switched off and will not cry at the seeming injustice of their fate. A business can move from using coal to natural gas without the neglected energy source walking off a cliff. But labour has a habit of meeting attempts to reduce its price or presence with emotion. It sobs in toilet cubicles, it drinks to ease its fears of under-achievement and it may choose death over redundancy.

These emotive responses point us to two imperatives coexisting within the arena in which status is accorded: an *economic imperative* which dictates that the primary task of business is to realize a profit. And a *human imperative* which leads employees to hunger for financial security, respect and tenure.

Though the two imperatives may for long periods coexist without apparent friction, what makes anxiety a lingering presence in the lives of all wage-dependent workers is the awareness that, in any serious choice between the two, it is the economic one that must always – by the very logic of the commercial system – prevail.

Struggles between labour and capital may no longer, in the developed world at least, be as bare-knuckled as in Marx's day. Yet, despite advances in working conditions and employment legislation, workers remain tools in a process in which their own happiness or economic well-being is necessarily incidental. Whatever camaraderie may build up between employer and employed, whatever goodwill workers may display and however many years they may have devoted to a task, they must live with the knowledge and attendant anxiety that their status is not guaranteed – that it remains dependent on both their own performance and the economic well-being of their organizations; that they are hence a means to profit, and never, as they might unshakeably long for at an emotional level, ends in themselves.

6

If such instability of employment matters, it is not only because of money. It is also, to return to our earliest theme, because of love, because work is the chief determinant of the amount of respect and care we will be granted. It is according to how we can answer the question of what we do – normally the first enquiry we will field in a new encounter – that the quality of our reception is likely to be decided.

And, unfortunately for our happiness, our capacity to provide a sufficiently elevated answer rarely lies securely in our province. It depends on the peaks and troughs of the economists' graphs, struggles in the market place and the vagaries of luck and of inspiration – while, for its part, our need for love remains un-wavering, no less steady or insistent than it might have been in infancy; an imbalance between our requirements and the uncertain conditions of the world that contributes a stubborn fifth pillar on which our status anxieties rest.

PART TWO

SOLUTIONS

I.
PHILOSOPHY

Honour and Vulnerability

1

In Hamburg in 1834, a handsome young army officer, Baron von Trautmansdorf, challenged a fellow officer, Baron von Ropp, to a duel over a poem that von Ropp had written and circulated among friends about von Trautmansdorf's moustache, stating that it was thin and floppy and hinting that this might not be the only part of von Trautmansdorf's physique imbued with such qualities. The feud between the barons had originated in their mutual passion for the same woman, Countess Lodoiska, the grey-green-eyed widow of a Polish general. Unable to resolve their differences amicably, the two men met in a field in a Hamburg suburb early on a March morning. Both were carrying swords, both were short of their thirtieth birthdays, both died in the ensuing fight.

The event was no exception. From its origins in Renaissance Italy until its end in the First World War, the practice of duelling claimed the lives of hundreds of thousands of Europeans. During the seventeenth century, in Spain alone it was responsible for 5,000 deaths. Visitors to the country were told to take extra care when addressing locals, lest they offend their honour and end up in a grave. 'Duels happen every day in Spain,' declared one character in a Calderón play. In France in 1608, Lord Herbert of Cherbury reported that there was 'scarce any man thought worth looking on, that had not killed some other in a duel', while in England it was widely held that no one could be a gentleman until he had 'taken up his sword'.

Though duels were at times sparked by matters of objective importance, the majority had their origins in small, even petty, questions of honour. In Paris in 1678, one man killed another who had described his apartment as tasteless. In Florence in 1702, a literary man ended the life of a cousin who had accused him of not understanding Dante. In France, under the regency of Philippe d'Orléans, two officers of the guard fought on the Quai des Tuileries over the ownership of an Angora cat.

2

Duelling symbolizes a radical incapacity to believe that our status might be our business, something we decide and do not revise according to the shifting judgements of our audience. For the dueller, what other people think of him will be the only factor in settling what he may think of himself. He cannot continue to be acceptable in his own eyes when those around him find him evil or dishonourable, a coward or a failure, a fool or an effeminate. So dependent is his self-image on the views of others that he would prefer to die by a bullet or stab wound than allow unfavourable ideas about him to remain lodged in the public mind.

Entire societies have made the maintenance of status and more particularly 'honour' a primary task of every adult male. In traditional Greek village society, honour was called *time*; in Muslim communities, *sharaf*; among Hindus, *izzat* – and in all cases, it was through violence that honour was expected to be upheld. In traditional Spanish communities, to be worthy of *honra* a man had to be physically brave, sexually potent, predatory towards women before he was married and loyal thereafter, able to look after his family financially and authoritative enough with his wife to ensure that she did not exchange flirtatious banter or sleep with other men. Dishonour flowed from one's own infringements of codes, but also from any failure to respond with sufficient violence to an *injuria* from another. If one was ridiculed in the market square or given an offensive look in the street, anything short of soliciting a fight would confirm the point of one's offenders.

3

Though we may look askance at those who resort to violence to answer questions of honour, we are liable to share the most significant aspect of the mindset of those who do so: an extreme vulnerability to the disdain of others. Like the most hot-headed of duellers, our self-esteem is likely to be determined by the value we are accorded by others. Duelling is only a helpfully far-fetched historical example of a more universal, thin-skinned emotional disposition towards matters of status.

An intense need to be viewed favourably by others has lost little of its hold on our sense of priorities. The fear of becoming what the Spanish termed a *deshonrado* or 'dishonoured one', a category whose contemporary connotations might best be captured by the chillingly contemptuous word 'loser', may haunt us no less than it did the characters of the tragedies of Calderón or Lope de Vega.

To be denied status – for example, because we have failed to reach certain professional goals or been unable to provide for our families – may prove as painful to us as it did to the members of a traditional community who had suffered a loss of *honra, tīmē, sharaf* or *izzat.*

Philosophy and Invulnerability

'Other people's heads are too wretched a place for
true happiness to have its seat.'
Schopenhauer, *Parerga and Paralipomena* (1851)

'Nature didn't tell me: "Don't be poor". Nor indeed:
"Be rich"; but she does beg me: "Be independent".'
Chamfort, *Maxims* (1795)

'It's not my place in society that makes me well off,
but my judgements; and these I can carry with me . . .
These alone are my own and can't be taken away.'
Epictetus, *Discourses* (*c.* AD 100)

1

In the Greek peninsula early in the fifth century BC, there emerged a
group of individuals, many of them with beards, who were singularly
free of the anxieties about status that tormented their contemporaries. These philosophers were untroubled by either the psychological or the material consequences of a humble position in society,
they remained calm in the face of insult, disapproval and penury.
When Socrates saw a pile of gold and jewellery being borne in
procession through the streets of Athens, he exclaimed, 'Look how
many things there are which I don't want.' When Alexander the Great
passed through Corinth, he visited the philosopher Diogenes and
found him sitting under a tree, dressed in rags, with no money to his
name. Alexander, the most powerful man in the world, asked if he
could do anything to help him. 'Yes,' replied the philosopher, 'if you
could step out of the way. You are blocking the sun.' Alexander's

soldiers were horrified, expecting an outburst of their commander's famous anger. But Alexander only laughed and remarked that if he were not Alexander, he would certainly like to be Diogenes. Antisthenes was told that a great many people in Athens had started to praise him. 'Why,' he answered, 'what have I done wrong?' Empedocles had a similar regard for the intelligence of others. He once lit a lamp in broad daylight and said, as he went around, 'I am looking for someone with a mind.' Having watched Socrates being insulted in the market place, a passer-by asked him, 'Don't you worry about being called names?' 'Why? Do you think I should resent it if an ass had kicked me?' replied Socrates.

2

It was not that these philosophers had ceased to pay any attention to a distinction between kindness and ridicule, success and failure. They had merely settled on a way of responding to the darker half of the equation that owed nothing to the traditional honour code, and its suggestion that what others think of us must determine what we can think of ourselves, and that every insult, whether accurate or not, must shame us.

Honour Relations

OTHERS' VIEW	SELF-IMAGE
You are dishonourable ⟶	I am dishonourable

Philosophy introduced a new element to the relationship with external opinion, what one might visualize as a box into which all public perceptions, whether positive or negative, would first have to be directed in order to be assessed, and then sent on to the self with renewed force if they were true, or ejected harmlessly into the atmosphere to be dispersed with a laugh or a shrug of the shoulders if they were false. The philosophers termed the box 'reason'.

Intellectual Conscience

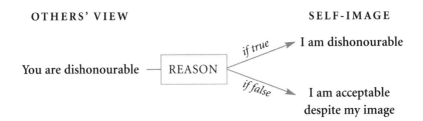

According to the rules of reason, a given conclusion is to be deemed true if, and only if, it flows from a logical sequence of thoughts founded on sound initial premises. Considering mathematics to be the model of good thinking, philosophers began to search for an approximation of its objective certainties in ethical life too. Thanks to reason, our status could – philosophers proposed – be settled according to an intellectual conscience, rather than being abandoned to the whims and emotions of the market square. And if rational examination revealed that we had been unfairly treated by the community, philosophers recommended that we be no more perturbed by the judgement than we would be if we had been approached by a deluded person bent on proving that two and two amounted to five.

Throughout his *Meditations* (AD 167), the emperor and philosopher Marcus Aurelius, moving in the unstable world of Roman politics, reminded himself to submit any views he heard about his character and achievements to reason before allowing them to affect his self-conception. '[Your decency] does not depend on the testimony of someone else,' insisted the philosopher-emperor, thereby challenging his society's faith in an honour-based assessment of people: 'Does what is praised become *better*? Does an emerald become *worse* if it isn't praised? And what of gold, ivory, a flower or a little plant?' Rather than being seduced by hearing his name well spoken of or retreating in pain when it was insulted, Marcus recommended taking his bearings from who he knew himself to be: 'Will any man despise me? Let him see to it. But I will see to it that I may not be found doing or saying anything that deserves to be despised.'

3

We should not deduce from this that the condemnation or censure of others is invariably undeserved. Leaving our assessment of our worth to an intellectual conscience is not to be confused with an expectation of unconditional love. Unlike parents or lovers, who may value us whatever we do and however great our faults, philosophers continue to apply criteria to their love, only not the shaky, unreasonable criteria that the wider world is in danger of resorting to. There may indeed be times when an intellectual conscience will demand that we be harsher on ourselves than others have been. Instead of rejecting a hierarchy of success and failure altogether, philosophy merely reconfigures the judging process, it lends legitimacy to the idea that the mainstream value system may be unfairly consigning some people to disgrace while perhaps equally unfairly consigning others to respectability – and in the case of an injustice, it helps us to hold on to the thought that we may be lovable even outside the halo of the praise of others.

4

Similarly, philosophy does not deny the utility of certain kinds of anxiety. As successful insomniacs have long emphasized, it may be the anxious who best survive.

Yet if we admit the worth of certain anxious feelings in helping us to find safety and develop our talents, we may be entitled to challenge the utility of other emotions in relation to precisely these same goals. We may feel envy about a condition or possession that would make us unhappy if we secured it. And we may experience ambitions unconnected to our real needs. Left to their own devices, our emotions are as likely to push us towards indulgence, un-controlled anger and self-destruction as towards health and virtue. Because it seems characteristic for these emotions either to under-shoot or overshoot their targets, philosophers have counselled that we use our reasoning faculties to guide them to an appropriate end, asking ourselves whether what we want is truly what we need and what we fear is truly what there is to be afraid of.

In his *Eudemian Ethics* (*c.* 350 BC), Aristotle offered examples of how human behaviour will, if left unexamined, typically err towards extremes and outlined an ideal or golden mean, as stolid as it is wise, towards which we should aim to direct it with the help of reason:

−	PHILOSOPHICAL IDEAL	+
Cowardice	Courage	Rashness
Stinginess	Liberality	Profligacy
Spinelessness	Gentleness	Rage
Boorishness	Wittiness	Buffoonery
Surliness	Friendliness	Obsequiousness

And, we might add:

Status lethargy	Ambition	Status hysteria

Intelligent Misanthropy

1

If we have listened to well-founded criticism of our behaviour, paid heed to targeted anxieties about our ambitions and adopted a proper sense of responsibility for our failures, and yet continue to be accorded low status by our community, we may be tempted to adopt an approach practised by some of the greatest philosophers of the Western tradition. We may, through an unparanoid understanding of the warps of the value system around us, settle for a stance of intelligent misanthropy, free of either defensiveness or pride.

2

When we begin to scrutinize the opinions of other people, philosophers have long proposed, we stand to make a discovery at once saddening and curiously releasing: that the views of the majority of the population on the majority of subjects are permeated with extraordinary confusion and error. Chamfort, echoing the misanthropic attitude of generations of philosophers before and after him, put the matter simply: 'Public opinion is the worst of all opinions.'

The reason for this defectiveness of opinion lies in the public's reluctance to submit its thoughts to the rigours of rational examination and its reliance on intuition, emotion and custom instead. 'One can be certain that every generally held idea, every received notion, will be an idiocy, because it has been able to appeal to a majority,' observed Chamfort, adding that what is flatteringly called common sense is usually little short of common nonsense, suffering as it does from simplification and illogicality, prejudice and shallowness: 'The most absurd customs and the most ridiculous ceremonies are everywhere excused by an appeal to the phrase, *but that's the tradition.* This is exactly what the Hottentots say when Europeans ask them why they eat grasshoppers and devour their body lice. *That's the tradition,* they explain.'

3

Though having to acknowledge the poverty of public opinion may be painful, the realization may nevertheless have helpful implications for our anxieties about status, for our exhausting desire to ensure that others think well of us and our thin-skinned longing for signs of love.

The approval of others could be said to matter to us for two reasons: materially, because the neglect of the community can bring with it physical discomfort and danger; and psychologically, because it can prove impossible to retain confidence in ourselves once others have ceased to accord us respect.

It is in relation to this second consequence of inattention that the benefits of a philosophical approach emerge, for rather than letting every case of opposition or neglect wound us, we are invited first to examine the justice of others' behaviour. Only that which is both damning *and* true should be allowed to shatter our esteem. We should halt the masochistic process whereby we seek the approval of people before we have asked ourselves whether their views deserve to be listened to; the process whereby we seek the love of those for whom we discover, once we study their minds, that we have scant respect.

We might then start unrancorously to disdain certain others as much as they disdain us – a misanthropic stance of which the history of philosophy is replete with the most fortifying examples.

4

'We will gradually become indifferent to what goes on in the minds of other people when we acquire an adequate knowledge of the superficial and futile nature of their thoughts, of the narrowness of their views, of the paltriness of their sentiments, of the perversity of their opinions, and of the number of their errors ... We shall then see that whoever attaches a lot of value to the opinions of others pays them too much honour,' argued Arthur Schopenhauer, a leading model of philosophical misanthropy.

In *Parerga and Paralipomena* (1851), the philosopher proposed that nothing could more quickly correct our desire to be liked by others than focusing on their true characters, which were, he reasoned, for the most part excessively brutish and stupid. 'In every country the principal entertainment of society has become card playing,' he pointed out. 'It is a measure of the worth of society and the declared bankruptcy of all ideas and thoughts.' Furthermore, these card players were usually sly and immoral: 'The term *coquin méprisable* [contemptible rogue] is alas applicable to an unholy number of people in this world.' And when they were not evil, people tended to be plain dull. Schopenhauer quoted with approval Voltaire's remark: '*La terre est couverte de gens qui ne méritent pas qu'on leur parle*' (the earth swarms with people who are not worth talking to).

Can we really take the opinions of such people so seriously? asked Schopenhauer. Can we really continue to let their verdicts govern what we make of ourselves? Can our self-esteem sensibly be surrendered to a group of card players? Even if these people do come to respect one, how much can this respect ever be worth? Or, as Schopenhauer put the question, 'Would a musician feel flattered by the loud applause of his audience if it were known to him that, with the exception of one or two, it consisted entirely of deaf people?'

5

The disadvantage of this otherwise usefully clear-eyed view of humanity is that it may leave us with few friends. Schopenhauer's fellow philosophical misanthrope Chamfort intimated the problem: 'Once we have resolved only to see those who will treat us morally and virtuously, reasonably and truthfully, without treating conventions, vanities and ceremonials as anything other than props of polite society; when we have taken this resolve (and we have to do so or we'll end up foolish, weak or villainous), the result is that we will have to live more or less on our own.'

Schopenhauer accepted the possibility with good grace. 'There is in the world only the choice between loneliness and vulgarity,' he confirmed and went on to advise that all young people should be taught 'how to put up with loneliness ... because the less a man is compelled to come into contact with others, the better off he is'. Fortunately, after spending some time working and living with people, anyone sensible will, suggested Schopenhauer, naturally feel 'as little inclined to frequent association with others as schoolmasters to join the games of the boisterous and noisy crowds of children who surround them'.

This said, a decision to avoid people shouldn't imply that one has no desire whatever for company. It may simply reflect a dissatisfaction with what is available. Cynics are only idealists with awkwardly high standards. In Chamfort's words: 'It is sometimes said of a man who lives alone that he does not like society. This is like saying of a man that he does not like going for walks because he is not fond of walking at night in the forêt de Bondy.'

6

From their isolated studies, philosophers have recommended that we follow our internal consciences rather than signs of approval or condemnation from outside. What matters is not what we *seem* to a random group, but what we *know* we are. In Schopenhauer's words: 'Every reproach can hurt only to the extent that it hits the mark. Whoever actually knows that he does not deserve a reproach can and will confidently treat it with contempt.'

To heed the misanthropic philosophical counsel, we should surrender our puerile concern for policing our own status – an impossible task that would in theory demand that we duel with, and end the life of, everyone who had ever held a negative opinion of us – in order to settle instead for the more solidly grounded satisfactions of a logically based sense of our worth.

II.
ART

Introduction

1

What is art good for? The question was in the air in Britain in the 1860s and, according to many commentators, the answer was: not very much. It wasn't art that had made the great industrial towns, laid the railways, dug the canals, expanded the empire and made Britain pre-eminent among nations. Indeed, art seemed capable of sapping the very qualities that had made these achievements possible; prolonged contact with it risked encouraging effeminacy, introspection, homosexuality, gout and defeatism. In a speech in 1865, John Bright, MP for Birmingham, described cultured people as a pretentious cabal whose only claim to distinction was 'a smattering of the two dead languages of Greek and Latin'. The Oxford academic Frederic Harrison held an equally caustic view of the benefits of prolonged communion with literature, history or painting. 'Culture is a desirable quality in a critic of new books, and sits well on a possessor of *belles lettres*,' he conceded, but 'as applied to everyday life or politics, it means simply a turn for small fault-finding, love of selfish ease, and indecision in action. The man of culture is one of the poorest mortals alive. For simple pedantry and want of good sense no man is his equal. No assumption is too unreal, no end is too unpractical for him.'

When these practically minded disparagers looked around for a representative of art's many deficiencies, they could find few more tempting targets on the English literary scene than the poet and critic Matthew Arnold, Professor of Poetry at Oxford and the author of several slim volumes of melancholic verse that had been well received among a highbrow coterie. Not only was Arnold in the habit of walking the streets of London with a silver-tipped cane, he also spoke in a quiet, high-pitched voice, sported peculiarly elongated sideburns, parted his hair in the middle and, worst of all, had the impudence to keep hinting, in a variety of newspaper articles and public lectures, that art might be one of the most important pursuits of life. This in an age when for the first time one could travel from London to Birmingham in a single morning and Britain had earned itself the title of workshop of the world. The *Daily Telegraph*, stout upholder of industry and monarchy, was infuriated. It dubbed Arnold an 'elegant Jeremiah' and 'the high-priest of the kid-gloved persuasion', and it mockingly accused him of trying to lure the hardworking, sensible people of the land 'to leave their shops and duties behind them in order to recite songs, sing ballads and read essays'.

2

Arnold accepted the ribbing with good grace until, in 1869, he was goaded into writing a systematic, book-length defence of what he believed art was for and why exactly it had such an important function to play in life – even for a generation that had witnessed the invention of the foldaway umbrella and the steam engine.

Arnold's *Culture and Anarchy* began by acknowledging some of the charges laid at art's door. In the eyes of many, it was nothing more, he said, than 'a scented salve for human miseries, a religion breathing a spirit of cultivated inaction, making its believers refuse to lend a hand at uprooting evils. It is often summed up as being not practical or – as some critics more familiarly put it – all moonshine.'

But far from moonshine, great art was, Arnold proposed, a medium that could offer solutions to life's deepest tensions and anxieties. However impractical art might seem to 'the young lions of the *Daily Telegraph*', it was capable of presenting us with nothing less than an interpretation of and solution to the deficiencies of existence.

Consider the work of any great artist, proposed Arnold, and you will find it marked (directly or not) by 'the desire to remove human error, clear human confusion, and diminish human misery'. All great artists are, said Arnold, imbued with 'the aspiration to leave the world better and happier than they find it'. They may not always embody such an aspiration in an overtly political message, they may not even be conscious of such an aspiration, and yet, within their work, there will almost always be a protest against the state of things and so an effort to correct our insights or to educate us to perceive beauty, to help us understand pain or to reignite our sensitivities, to nurture our capacity for empathy or to rebalance our moral perspective through sadness or laughter. Arnold concluded his argument with a pronouncement upon which this chapter is built. Art, said Arnold, is 'the criticism of life'.

3

What should we understand by the phrase? Perhaps first, and most obvious, that life is a phenomenon in need of criticism, that we are, as fallen creatures, in permanent danger of worshipping false gods, of failing to understand ourselves or misinterpreting the behaviour of others, of growing unproductively anxious or desirous, and of losing ourselves to vanity and error. Surreptitiously and beguilingly, with humour or gravity, works of art – novels, poems, plays, paintings or films – can function as vehicles to explain our condition to us. They may act as guides to a truer, more judicious, more intelligent understanding of the world.

Given that few things are more in need of criticism (or insight and analysis) than our approach to status and its distribution, it is hardly surprising to find so many artists across time creating works that in some way contest the methods by which people are accorded a rank in society. The history of art is filled with challenges – ironic, angry, lyrical, sad or amusing – to the status system.

Art and Snobbery

1

Jane Austen began work on *Mansfield Park* in the spring of 1813 and published it the following year. The novel tells the story of Fanny Price, a shy, modest young girl from a penniless family in Portsmouth who, in order to relieve her parents, is asked by her aunt and uncle, the plutocratic Sir Thomas and Lady Bertram, to come to Mansfield Park, their stately home, to live with them and their four children. The Bertrams stand at the pinnacle of the English county hierarchy, they are spoken of with awe and reverence by their neighbours; their coquettish teenage daughters, Maria and Julia, enjoy a generous clothes allowance and have both been given their own horses; and their eldest son, Tom, bumptious and casually insensitive, spends his time in London clubs, lubricating his friendships with champagne while focusing his hopes for the future on his father's death and the inheritance of an estate and title. Though adept at the self-deprecating manners of the English upper classes, Sir Thomas Bertram and his family never forget (and do not allow others to forget) their superior rank and all the distinction that must naturally accompany their ownership of a large landscaped garden upon which deer wander during the quiet hours between tea and dinner.

Fanny may have come to live under the same roof as the Bertrams, but she cannot be on an equal footing with them. Her privileges have been given to her at the discretion of Sir Thomas, her cousins patronize her, the neighbours view her with a mixture of suspicion and pity and she is treated by most of the family like a lady-in-waiting whose company one enjoys but whose feelings one is fortunately never under any prolonged obligation to consider.

Before Fanny arrives in Mansfield Park, Austen allows us to eavesdrop on the family's anxieties about their new charge. '"I hope she will not tease my poor pug,"' remarks Lady Bertram. The children wonder what Fanny's clothes will be like, whether she will speak French and know the names of the kings and queens of England. Sir Thomas Bertram, in spite of having proffered the invitation to Fanny's parents, expects the worst: '"We shall probably see much to wish altered in her and should prepare ourselves for gross ignorance, some meanness of opinions and a very distressing vulgarity of manner."' His sister-in-law Mrs Norris states that Fanny must early on be told that she is not, and never will be, *one of them.* Sir Thomas avers, '"We must make her remember that she is not a *Miss Bertram.* I should wish to see Fanny and her cousins very good friends but they cannot be equals. Their rank, fortune, rights and expectations will always be different."'

Fanny's arrival seems only to confirm the family's prejudices against those who have failed to grow up on estates with landscaped gardens. Julia and Maria discover that Fanny has only one nice dress, speaks no French and doesn't know anything. '"Only think, my cousin cannot put the map of Europe together,"' Julia tells her aunt and mother, '"nor can she tell the principal rivers in Russia and she has never heard of Asia Minor – How strange! Did you ever hear anything so stupid? Do you know, we asked her last night which way she would go to get to Ireland and she said, she should cross to the Isle of Wight." "Yes, my dear," replies Mrs Norris, "but you and your sister are blessed with wonderful memories, and your poor cousin has probably none at all. You must make allowances for her and pity her deficiency."'

Jane Austen, however, takes a little longer to make up her mind about who is deficient and in what capacity. For a decade or more, she follows Fanny patiently along the corridors and reception rooms of Mansfield Park, she listens to her on her walks around the gardens and in her bedroom, she reads her letters, she eavesdrops on her observations of her family, she watches the movements of her eyes and mouth; she peers into her soul. And in the process she picks up on a rare, quiet virtue.

Unlike Julia or Maria, Fanny is not concerned with whether a young man has a large house and a title, she is offended by her cousin Tom's casual cruelty and arrogance, she flinches from her aunt's financial considerations of her neighbours. Meanwhile Fanny's relatives, ranked so highly in the standard county status hierarchy, are more troublingly placed in that other status system: the novelist's hierarchy of preference. Maria and her suitor, Mr Rushworth, may have horses, houses and inheritances, but Jane Austen has seen how they fell in love and she does not forget it:

'Mr Rushworth was from the first struck with the beauty of Miss Bertram, and being inclined to marry, soon fancied himself in love. Being now in her twenty-first year, Maria Bertram was beginning to think matrimony a duty; and as a marriage with Mr Rushworth would give her the enjoyment of a larger income than her father's, as well as ensure her a house in town, it became her evident duty to marry Mr Rushworth if she could.'

Who's Who or *Debrett's Guide to the Top Families of England* might have held Maria and Mr Rushworth in high esteem. After such a paragraph, Austen cannot – nor will she let her readers. The novelist exchanges the standard lens through which people are viewed in society, a lens which magnifies wealth and power, for a moral lens, which magnifies qualities of character. Through this lens, the high and mighty may become small, the forgotten and re-tiring figures may loom large. Within the world of the novel, virtue is shown to be spread without regard to material wealth. The rich and well-mannered are not immediately good or the poor and unschooled bad. Goodness may lie with the lame ugly child, the destitute porter, the hunchback in the attic or the girl ignorant of the first facts of geography. Certainly Fanny has no elegant dresses, has no money and can't speak French, but by the end of *Mansfield Park* she has been revealed as the one possessed of a noble soul, while the other members of her family, despite their titles and accomplishments, have fallen into moral confusion. Sir Thomas Bertram has allowed snobbery to ruin the education of his children, his daughters have married for money and paid an emotional price for their decision, and his wife has let her heart turn to stone. The hierarchical system of Mansfield Park has been turned on its head.

But Austen does not simply assert her concept of true hierarchy with the bluntness of a preacher, she enlists our sympathies for it and marshals our abhorrence for its opposite with the skill and humour of a great novelist. She does not *tell* us why her sense of priorities is important, she *shows* us why within the context of a story which also happens to make us laugh and grips us enough that we want to finish supper early to read on. As we reach the end of *Mansfield Park* we are invited to go back into the world from which Austen has drawn us aside and respond to others as she has taught us, to pick up on and recoil from greed, arrogance and pride and to be drawn to goodness within ourselves and others.

Austen modestly and famously described her art as 'the little bit (two inches wide) of ivory on which I work with so fine a brush, as produces little effect after much labour', but her novels are suffused with greater ambitions. Her art is an attempt, through what she called a study of 'three or four families in a country village', to criticize and so alter our lives.

2

Austen was not alone in her ambitions. In almost every great novel of the nineteenth and twentieth centuries we find an assault on, or scepticism towards, the standard social hierarchy, and a redefinition of precedence according to moral qualities rather than financial assets or bloodlines. The heroes and heroines of fiction are only on rare occasions those to whom *Debrett's* or *Who's Who* would give priority. The first become something like the last, the last something like the first. In Balzac's *Le Père Goriot* (1834), it is not Madame de Nucingen, with her gilded house, towards whom our sympathies are guided, it is to old toothless Goriot, eking out his days in a putrid boarding house. In Hardy's *Jude the Obscure* (1895), it is not the Oxford dons we respect, it is the impoverished, ill-schooled stone-mason repairing the gargoyles of the university's colleges.

By standing witness to hidden lives, novels may act as imaginative counterweights to dominant conceptions of hierarchy. They can reveal that the maid busying herself with lunch is a creature of rare sensitivity and moral greatness, while the heart of the baron who laughs raucously and owns a silver mine is withered and acrid.

If we are inclined to forget the lesson, it is in part because what is best in other people only rarely has the chance to express itself in the sort of external achievements that attract and hold our ordinary, vagabond attention. George Eliot begins *Middlemarch* (1872) with a discussion of this tendency to admire only obvious exploits, drawing an unlikely comparison between the status of her heroine and that of St Teresa of Avila (1512-82). Because of luck and circumstance, because she came from a wealthy and well-connected family, St Teresa was – Eliot reminds us – able to embody her goodness and creativity in concrete acts. She founded seventeen convents, she communicated with the most devout minds of her age, she wrote an autobiography and a number of treatises on prayer and vision, she became one of the principal saints of the Roman Catholic Church and one of its greatest mystics. By the time of her death, Teresa's status reflected the virtues of her character. But George Eliot goes on to remind us of the number of people in the world no less intelligent or creative than the Spanish saint who nevertheless

Status in Life - Status in Novels

NOVEL	HIGH STATUS IN NOVEL, LOW STATUS IN LIFE	HIGH STATUS IN LIFE, LOW STATUS IN NOVEL
Joseph Andrews (1742) Henry Fielding	Joseph Andrews Parson Adams	Lady Booby Parson Trulliber
Vanity Fair (1848) William Thackeray	William Dobbin Amelia Sedley	Becky Sharp Jos Sedley George Osborne Sir Pitt Crawley Rawdon Crawley
Bleak House (1853) Charles Dickens	Esther Summerson Jo Bucket	The Dedlocks Mr Chadband Mrs Jellyby Richard Carstone
The Woman in White (1860) Wilkie Collins	Anne Catherick Marian Halcombe	Sir Percival Glyde Count Fosco Frederick Fairlie
The Way We Live Now (1875) Anthony Trollope	Paul Montague Mr Brehgert John Crumb	Augustus Melmotte Marie Melmotte Sir Felix Carbury Dolly Longestaffe Georgiana Longestaffe Lord Nidderdale

fail to externalize their qualities in great actions, through a combination of their own errors and unhelpful social conditions, and who are therefore condemned to bear a status with scant relation to their inner selves. 'Many Teresas have been born who found for themselves no epic life; only a life of mistakes, the offspring of a certain spiritual grandeur ill-matched with a meanness of opportunity,' writes Eliot. It is the life of one such woman, Dorothea Brooke, living in an English town in the first half of the nineteenth century, that *Middlemarch* sets out to recount, the novel offering a critique of the world's habit of neglecting what Eliot calls 'spiritual grandeur' whenever it is unlinked to 'long-recognized deeds'.

Dorothea may have many of the virtues of St Teresa, but they are not visible to a world attentive only to the symbols of status. Because she marries a sickly clergyman and then, little more than a year after his death, gives up her estate to marry her late husband's cousin (who has no property and is not well born), society insists that Dorothea cannot be a 'good woman', it gossips about her and shuns her company. 'Certainly those determining acts of her life were not ideally beautiful,' Eliot concedes. 'They were the mixed result of a young and noble impulse struggling amidst the conditions of an imperfect social state.' However, in some of the most quietly stirring lines in English nineteenth-century fiction, Eliot asks us to look beyond Dorothea's socially unacceptable marriage and her lack of achievements in order to recognize that, in a domestic and circumscribed way, her character is no less saintly than St Teresa of Avila's: 'Her finely-touched spirit had its fine issues, even though they were not widely visible. Her full nature spent itself in channels which had no great name on the earth. But the effect of her being on those around her was incalculably diffusive: for the growing good of the world is partly dependent on unhistoric acts; and that things are not so ill with you and me as they might have been, is half owing to the number who lived faithfully a hidden life and rest in unvisited tombs.'

These are lines that may be stretched to define a whole conception of the novel: an artistic medium to help us understand and appreciate the value of every hidden life that rests in an unvisited tomb. 'If art does not enlarge men's sympathies, it does nothing morally,' knew George Eliot.

In Zadie Smith's *White Teeth* (2000), we meet Samad, a middle-aged Bangladeshi employed as a waiter in an Indian restaurant. He is treated roughly by his superiors, works until three in the morning and has to wait upon coarse customers who magnanimously reward him with fifteen-pence tips for his services. Samad dreams of recovering his dignity, of escaping the material and psychological consequences of his status. He longs to alert others to the riches within himself, unapparent to customers, who barely look up when he takes their order ('Go Bye Ello Sag, please' and 'Chicken Jail Fret See wiv Chips, fanks'). He imagines wearing a sign around his neck, a white placard that would read in letters large enough for the whole world to see:

> I AM NOT A WAITER. I HAVE BEEN A STUDENT, A SCIENTIST, A SOLDIER, MY WIFE IS CALLED ALSANA, WE LIVE IN EAST LONDON BUT WE WOULD LIKE TO MOVE NORTH. I AM A MUSLIM BUT ALLAH HAS FORSAKEN ME OR I HAVE FORSAKEN ALLAH, I'M NOT SURE. I HAVE A FRIEND – ARCHIE – AND OTHERS. I AM FORTY-NINE BUT WOMEN STILL TURN IN THE STREET. SOMETIMES.

He never acquires such a placard, but he gets the next best thing, a novelist who provides him with a voice, the whole novel in which Samad appears being in a sense a giant placard that will help to make it ever so slightly harder for its readers to order Chicken Jail Fret See in a casually indifferent, casually dehumanizing way again. On reading the novel our sympathies will have been expanded; the history of the novel being perhaps nothing more than one long procession of placards that tell the world:

I AM NOT JUST A WAITER, A DIVORCEE, AN ADULTERER, A THIEF, AN UNEDUCATED MAN, A PECULIAR CHILD, A MURDERER, A CONVICT, A FAILURE AT SCHOOL OR A SHY PERSON WITH NOTHING TO SAY FOR HERSELF.

3

Paintings too can challenge the world's normal understanding of who and what is important.

Jean-Baptiste Chardin painted his *Meal for a Convalescent* in 1746. A plainly dressed woman stands in a sparsely furnished room, patiently peeling an egg for a sick person we cannot see. It is an ordinary moment in the life of an ordinary person. Why paint such a thing? For much of Chardin's career his critics agreed with the sceptical tenor of the question. He was a gifted painter who had mysteriously decided to devote his attention to loaves of bread, broken plates, knives and forks, apples and pears, as well as working- or lower-middle-class characters going about their business in plain kitchens and living rooms.

This was certainly not what a great artist was supposed to paint, according to the rules of art prescribed by the French Academy of Painting. Upon its foundation by Louis XIV in 1648, the Academy had arranged the different genres of painting into a hierarchy of importance. At the head of this came history paintings: canvases expressing the nobility of ancient Greece and Rome or depicting biblical morality tales. Second came portraits, especially of kings and queens. Third came landscapes, and only last came what were dismissively described as 'genre scenes', domestic lives of non-noble people. The artistic hierarchy directly matched the social hierarchy

Jean-Baptiste Chardin, Meal for a Convalescent, *1746*

of the world beyond the artists' studios, where a king on a horse surveying his estates was deemed naturally superior to a modestly dressed woman peeling an egg.

But within Chardin's art lay an implicit subversion of any vision of life that could dismiss as valueless a woman's domestic care, or indeed a piece of old pottery catching the afternoon sun ('Chardin has taught us that a pear can be as full of life as a woman, that a jug is as beautiful as a precious stone', Marcel Proust).

We find a handful of fellow spirits to Chardin in the history of painting, a handful of great correctives to our customary notions of importance. For example, the Welsh painter Thomas Jones, who worked in Italy, first in Rome and then in Naples, between 1776 and 1783. It was in Naples, in early April 1782, that Jones completed what may be two of the greatest oil on paper paintings in Western art, *Rooftops, Naples* (which hangs in the Ashmolean Museum in Oxford) and *Buildings in Naples* (in the National Museum of Wales, Cardiff).

The scenes Jones depicts are familiar from many Mediterranean towns, where houses are pressed together along narrow streets and give out on to the naked flanks of neighbouring buildings. In the heat of a warm afternoon, the streets tend to be quiet and the windows half shuttered. One may glimpse the outline of a woman moving inside one room and of a man sleeping in another. Occasionally, there may be the cry of a child, or the rustle of an old woman hanging laundry on a terrace with a rusting handrail.

Jones shows us the intense light of the south meeting walls of chipped and weathered stucco, the light bringing out every indentation and fracture and evoking the passage of time as effectively as the rough, weathered hands of a fisherman; time during which the seasons will have revolved, blank dead summer heat giving way to furious winter storms which, after an apparent eternity, will have ceded a place to tentative spring sunshine. Jones's stone and stucco reveal their kinship with clay and plaster and the fragments of pitted

rock on Mediterranean hillsides. The confusion of buildings affords us an impression of a town in which a multiplicity of lives is unfolding – in every window, lives no less complicated than those depicted in the great novels, lives of passion, boredom, playfulness and despair.

How seldom we notice rooftops; how easily our eyes are drawn to the more flamboyant attractions of a Roman temple or Renaissance church. Jones holds up the ignored scene for our contemplation and renders its latent beauty visible, so that never again will southern rooftops count for nothing in our understanding of happiness.

The Danish nineteenth-century painter Christen Købke was a

Thomas Jones, Rooftops, Naples, *1782*

third great artist with a subversive notion of what we should consider valuable. Between 1832 and 1838, Købke travelled around the suburbs, streets and gardens of his native Copenhagen. He painted a couple of cows ruminating in a field on a summer's afternoon. He caught two men and their wives on the shores of a lake, disembarking from their small sailing boat on an evening where night appears in no hurry to settle over the land, and lets an echo of daylight hover for an apparent eternity in the vast sky (in which a moon may have just appeared), a light that presages a gentle night, where one will be able to leave the windows open or sleep outside on blankets on the grass. He captured the view from the roof of Frederiksborg Castle,

Thomas Jones, Buildings in Naples, *1782*

looking out on to a neat patchwork of fields, gardens and farms; an image of an ordered community content with the snatched pleasures of ordinary life.

As in the work of Chardin and Jones, there is a challenge embedded in Købke's art to prevailing material ideas of what is important. The three artists seem to suggest that if the sky on a summer's evening, a pitted wall heated by the sun or an unknown woman peeling an egg for a sick person are truly among the loveliest sights we can hope to lay our eyes on, then we will have to doubt the value of much that we have been taught to respect and aspire to.

It may appear far-fetched to hang a quasi-political programme

Christen Købke, View from the Embankment of Lake Sortedam, *1838*

Christen Købke, The Roof of Frederiksborg Castle, *1834–5*

on a jug on a sideboard or a cow in a field, but the moral of a work by Købke, Jones or Chardin may stretch dauntingly far from that which we are ordinarily prepared to attribute to pieces of painted cloth or paper. Like Jane Austen or George Eliot, the great artists of everyday life may help us to correct a range of snobbish conceptions of what there is to esteem and honour in the world.

Christen Købke, A View in the Neighbourhood of the Lime Kiln, *1834–5*

Tragedy

1

The fear of failing at tasks would perhaps not be so great were it not for an awareness of how often failure tends to be harshly viewed and interpreted by others. Fear of the material consequences of failure is compounded by fear of the unsympathetic attitude of the world towards failure, of its haunting proclivity to refer to those who have failed as 'losers' – a word callously signifying both that people have lost and that they have at the same time forfeited any right to sympathy for having done so.

So unforgiving is the tone in which the majority of ruined lives is discussed that if the protagonists of many works of art – Oedipus, Antigone, Lear, Othello, Emma Bovary, Anna Karenina, Hedda Gabler or Tess – had had their destinies chewed over by a cabal of colleagues or old school acquaintances, they would have been unlikely to emerge well from the process. They might have fared even less well if the newspapers had come across them:

Othello:	'Love-crazed Immigrant Kills Senator's Daughter'
Madame Bovary:	'Shopaholic Adulteress Swallows Arsenic After Credit Fraud'
Oedipus the King:	'Sex with Mum was Blinding'

If there is something incongruous about these headlines, it is because we are used to thinking of the subjects they refer to as inherently complex, naturally deserving of a solemn and respectful attitude rather than the prurient and damning one which newspapers rarely hesitate to accord their victims.

But, in truth, there is nothing about these subjects to make them inevitable objects of concern and respect. That the legendary failed characters of art seem noble to us has little to do with their qualities *per se* and almost everything to do with the way we have been taught to consider them by their creators and chroniclers.

There is one art form in particular which has, since its inception, dedicated itself to recounting stories of great failure without recourse to mockery or judgement. While not absolving people of responsibility for their actions, its achievement has been to offer to those involved in catastrophes – disgraced statesmen, murderers, the bankrupt, emotional compulsives – a level of sympathy owed, but rarely paid, to every human.

2

Tragic art began in the theatres of ancient Greece in the sixth century BC and followed a hero, usually a high-born one, a king or a famous warrior, from prosperity and acclaim to ruin and shame, through some error of his own. The way the story was told was likely to leave members of an audience at once hesitant to condemn the hero for what had befallen him and humbled by a recognition of how easily they too might one day be ruined if ever they were presented with a situation similar to that with which the hero had been faced. The tragedy would leave them sorrowful before the difficulties of leading a good life and modest before those who had failed at the undertaking.

If the newspaper, with its language of perverts and weirdos, failures and losers, lies at one end of the spectrum of understanding, then it is tragedy that lies at the other – tragedy embodying an attempt to build bridges between the guilty and the apparently blameless, challenging our ordinary conceptions of responsibility, standing as the most psychologically sophisticated, most respectful account of how a human being may be dishonoured without at the same time forfeiting the right to be heard.

3

In his *Poetics* (*c.* 350 BC), Aristotle attempted to define the core constituents of an effective tragedy. There needed to be one central character, he said, the action had to unfold in a relatively compressed space of time and, unsurprisingly, 'the change in the hero's fortunes' had to be 'not from misery to happiness' but on the contrary 'from happiness to misery'.

But there were two other, more telling, requirements. A tragic hero had to be someone who was neither especially good nor especially bad, an everyday, ordinary kind of human being at the ethical level, someone we could relate to with ease, a person who combined a range of good qualities with certain defects, perhaps excessive pride or anger or impulsiveness. This character would then make a spectacular mistake, not from any profoundly evil motive, but from what Aristotle termed in Greek a *hamartia* or lapse of judgement, a temporary blindness, or a factual or emotional slip. And from this would flow the most terrible *peripeteia* or reversal of fortune, in the course of which the hero would lose everything he held dear and almost certainly pay with his life.

Pity for the hero, and fear for oneself based on an identification with him, would be the natural emotional outcome of following such a tale. The tragic work would educate us to acquire modesty about our capacity to avoid disaster and at the same time guide us to feel sympathy for those who had met with it. We were to leave the theatre disinclined ever again to adopt an easy, superior tone towards the fallen and the failed.

Aristotle's insight is that the sympathy we feel for the fiascos of others almost always has its origins in a palpable sense of how easily we too might, under certain circumstances, be involved in a calamity like theirs; just as our sympathy diminishes in proportion to the degree in which their actions come to seem as if they lie outside the range of our possibilities. How would a sane, normal person do *that*, we may feel upon hearing of characters who have married rashly, slept with members of their own families, murdered their lovers in jealous frenzies, lied to employers, stolen money or allowed an avaricious streak to ruin their careers. Confident of a cast-iron wall separating our nature and situation from theirs, comfortable in the well-worn saddle of our high horse, our capacity for tolerance is replaced by coldness and derision.

But the tragedian draws us close to an almost unbearable truth: that every folly of which a human being has been guilty in the course of history can be traced back to aspects of our own nature; that we bear within ourselves the whole of the human condition, in its worst and best aspects, so that we too might be capable of anything under the right, or rather the very wrong, circumstances. Once an audience has been brought close to this fact, they may willingly dismount from their high horses and feel their powers of sympathy and humility enhanced; they may accept how easily their own lives could be shattered if certain of their more regrettable character traits, which had until then led them to no serious accident, were one day to come into contact with a situation that allowed these flaws an unlimited and catastrophic reign – leaving them no less shamed and wretched than the unfortunate character suffering beneath the headline 'Sex with Mum was Blinding'.

4

The play that most perfectly suited Aristotle's conception of the tragic art form was Sophocles' *Oedipus the King*, first performed in Athens at the Festival of Dionysus in the spring of 430 BC.

Sophocles' hero, Oedipus, King of Thebes, is worshipped by his people for his benevolent rule and for having outwitted the Sphinx, who had menaced the city many years before, an exploit for which he had been rewarded with the throne. All the same, the king is not flawless. He is impetuous and prone to rage. Many years before the beginning of the play, one outburst had led him to kill an obstinate old man who had refused to get out of his way on the road into Thebes. However, the incident had largely been forgotten, because it had rapidly been followed by Oedipus' victory over the Sphinx, a period of prosperity and security for the city, as well as Oedipus' marriage to the beautiful Jocasta, widow of his predecessor, King Laius, who had died in unexplained circumstances in a fight with a young man on the road into Thebes.

Yet, as the play opens, a new disaster has descended upon the city. A peculiar plague, for which no cure can be found, is ravaging the population. Desperate, the subjects turn to their royal family for help. Oedipus' brother-in-law, Creon, is dispatched to seek answers from the oracle of Apollo at Delphi, which gnomically explains that the city is being punished for an unclean thing within it. Creon and others at court decide this must be an allusion to the unsolved murder of the previous monarch. Oedipus agrees and vows that he will personally see to it that the killer is found and punished without remorse.

Jocasta's face darkens as she hears this. As if for the first time, she remembers another prophecy from long ago: that her first husband, Laius, would be killed by his own son. To prevent the danger, when she and the old king had had a boy, the baby had been taken to a mountainside and left to die. However, the shepherd who had been charged with the task had taken pity on the child and given it to the King of Corinth for adoption instead. When this boy had reached maturity, an oracle had revealed to the king and queen that their son would kill his father and marry his mother. Oedipus had therefore left the city to travel the length of Greece, ending up in Thebes, of which he had become the ruler after he had outwitted the Sphinx – and, in a regrettable incident, an obstinate old man who had blocked his way on a road into the city.

Jocasta, the first to recognize what has happened, retires to her rooms in the royal palace and hangs herself. Oedipus finds her swinging from the rafters, cuts down her body and pierces his own eyes with the brooch from her dress. He embraces his two daughters, Ismene and Antigone, too young to understand the catastrophe in which their parents are involved, and sends himself into exile, to wander the earth in shame until his death.

5

We might make the rejoinder that killing our fathers and marrying our mothers are hardly errors of judgement many of us are likely to make. But the extraordinary dimensions of Oedipus' *hamartia* do not detract from the more universal features of the play. Oedipus' story affects us in so far as it reflects shocking aspects of our own character and condition: the way apparently small errors can have the gravest of consequences, our ignorance as to the effect of our actions, our tendency to presume that we are in conscious command of our destinies; the speed with which everything we love may be lost; and the unknown obscure forces, what Sophocles termed 'fate', against which our weak powers of reason and foresight are pitted. Oedipus had not been devoid of error. He had hubristically believed himself to have escaped the oracle's prophecies and had lazily accepted his subjects' high estimation. His pride and hot temper had led him to pick a fight with King Laius and an emotional cowardice had prevented him from connecting this murder to the prophecies. His self-righteousness had made him ignore the crime for many years and then blame Creon for hinting at his guilt.

Yet even if Oedipus bears responsibility for his fate, the tragic work renders easy condemnation of him untenable. It apportions blame to him without denying him sympathy. As Aristotle imagined, members of the audience will leave the auditorium appalled yet compassionate, haunted by the universal implications of the concluding message of the play's chorus:

People of Thebes, my countrymen, look on Oedipus.
He solved the famous riddle with his brilliance,
He rose to power, a man beyond all power.
Who could behold his greatness without envy?
Now what a black sea of terror has overwhelmed him.
Now as we keep our watch and wait the final day,
Count no man happy till he dies, free of pain at last.

6

If a tragic work allows us to experience a degree of concern for others' failure so much greater than that we ordinarily feel, it is principally because it leads us to plumb the origins of failure. In this context, to know more is necessarily to understand and to forgive more. A tragic work leads us artfully through the minuscule, often innocent, steps connecting a hero or heroine's prosperity to their downfall, and the perverse relationship between intentions and results. In the process we are unlikely to retain for long the indifferent or vengeful tone we might have had recourse to had we merely read the bare bones of a story of failure in a newspaper.

In the summer of 1848, a terse item appeared in many newspapers across Normandy. A twenty-seven-year-old woman named Delphine Delamare, née Couturier, living in the small town of Ry, not far from Rouen, had become dissatisfied with the routines of married life, had run up huge debts on superfluous clothes and household goods, had begun an affair and, under emotional and financial pressure, had taken her own life by swallowing arsenic. Madame Delamare left behind a young daughter and a distraught husband, Eugène Delamare, who had studied medicine in Rouen before taking up his post as a health officer in Ry, where he was loved by his clients and respected by the community.

One of those reading the newspaper was a twenty-seven year old aspiring novelist, Gustave Flaubert. The story of Madame Delamare stayed with him, it became something of an obsession, it followed him on a journey around Egypt and Palestine until, in September 1851, he settled down to work on *Madame Bovary*, published in Paris six years later.

One of the many things that happened when Madame Delamare, the adulteress from Ry, turned into Madame Bovary, the adulteress from Yonville, was that her life ceased to bear the dimensions of a black-and-white morality tale. As a newspaper story the case of Delphine Delamare had been seized upon by provincial conservative commentators as an example of the decline of respect for marriage among the young, of the increasing commercialization of society and of the loss of religious values. But to Flaubert art was the very antithesis of crass moralism. It was a realm in which human motives and behaviour could for once be explored in a depth that made a mockery of any attempt to construe saints or sinners. Readers of Flaubert's novel could observe Emma's naïve ideas of love, but also see where these had come from: they followed her into her child-hood, they read over her shoulder at her convent, they sat with her and her father during long summer afternoons in Tostes, in a kitchen where the sound of pigs and chickens drifted in from the yard. They watched her and Charles falling into an ill-matched marriage. They saw how Charles had been seduced by his loneliness and by a young woman's physical charms, and how Emma had been impelled by her desire to escape a cloistered life and by her lack of experience of men outside third-rate romantic literature. Readers could sympathize with Charles's complaints against Emma and Emma's complaints against Charles. Flaubert seemed almost deliberately to enjoy unsettling readers' desire to find comfortable answers. No sooner had he presented Emma in a positive light than he would undercut her with an ironic remark. But then, as readers were losing patience with her, as they felt her to be nothing more than a selfish hedonist, he would draw them back to her, would tell them something about her sensitivity that would make them cry. By the time Emma had lost her status in her community, had crammed arsenic into her mouth and lain down in her bedroom to await her death, few readers would be in a mood to judge.

We end Flaubert's novel with fear and sadness at how we have been made to live before we can begin to know how, at how limited our understanding of ourselves and others is, at how great and catastrophic are the consequences of our actions, and at how pitiless and uncompromising our community can be in response to our errors.

7

As readers or members of the audience of a tragic work, we are as far as it is possible to be from the spirit of the headline 'Shopaholic Adulteress Swallows Arsenic'. Tragedy inspires us to abandon ordinary life's simplified perspective on failure and defeat, and renders us generous towards the foolishness and transgressions endemic to our nature.

A world in which people had imbibed the lessons implicit within tragic art would be one in which the consequences of our failures would necessarily cease to weigh upon us so heavily.

Comedy

1

The summer of 1831 found King Louis-Philippe of France in a confident mood. The political and economic chaos of the July Revolution, which had brought him to power the year before, was giving way to prosperity and order. He had in place a competent team of officials led by his prime minister, Casimir Périer; he had travelled around the northern and eastern parts of his realm and been given a hero's welcome by the provincial middle classes. He lived in splendour in the Palais-Royal in Paris; banquets were thrown in his honour every week; he loved eating (especially *foie gras* and game); he had a vast personal fortune and a loving wife and children.

Ary Scheffer, King Louis-Philippe of France, *1835*

But there was one thing to cloud Louis-Philippe's composure. In late 1830, a twenty-eight-year-old unknown artist by the name of Charles Philipon had launched a satirical magazine, *La Caricature*, in which he had represented the head of the king, whom he accused of corruption and incompetence on a grand scale, in the shape of a pear. Not only did Philipon's cartoons allude unkindly to the king's swollen cheeks and bulbous forehead, the French word *poire*, meaning fathead or mug, neatly indicated a less than respectful attitude towards Louis-Philippe's powers of administration.

The king was enraged. He instructed his agents to obstruct the magazine's production and buy up all copies from Parisian kiosks. When this failed to deter Philipon, in November 1831 the caricaturist was charged with having 'caused offence to the person of the king' and ordered to appear in court in Paris. Speaking before a packed chamber, Philipon thanked the prosecutors for arresting a dangerous man like himself, but pointed out that the government had been negligent in their pursuit of the king's detractors. It should be a priority to try to arrest anything in the shape of a pear, even pears themselves should be locked up. There were thousands of them on trees all over France, every one of these fruits a criminal fit for incarceration, mocked Philipon. The court was not amused. He was sent to prison for six months, and when he repeated the pear joke in a new magazine, *Le*

Charivari, the following year, he was put straight back in jail – spending, in all, two years behind bars for drawing the monarch as a piece of fruit.

Three decades previously, Napoleon Bonaparte, then the most powerful man in Europe, had felt no less vulnerable before a sense of humour. On coming to power in 1799, he had ordered the closure of every satirical paper in Paris and told his police chief, Joseph Fouché, that he would not tolerate cartoonists taking liberties with his appearance. He preferred to leave his visual representation to Jacques-Louis David. He had asked the great painter to depict him leading his armies across the Alps, looking heroic on a horse. So pleased was he with the result, *Napoleon Crossing the Saint-Bernard* (1801), that he returned to David and asked him to paint the apogee of his triumphs, his coronation in Notre Dame in December 1804. It was an occasion of high pomp. All the grandees of France were gathered in the cathedral, Pope Pius VII was in attendance, representatives from most European countries came to pay their respects and music was especially composed by Jean-François Lesueur.

Blessing Napoleon, the pope called out across a hushed cathedral, '*Vivat imperator in aeternam*'. David completed his rendition of the scene, *Le Sacre de Joséphine,* in November 1807 and offered it 'to my illustrious master'. Napoleon was jubilant, he made David an officer of the Legion of Honour 'for services to art' and told him, as he pinned a medal to his chest, 'You have brought good taste back to France.'

But not all artists saw Napoleon as David did. A few years before *Le Sacre de Joséphine*, the English caricaturist James Gillray had drawn much the same scene, entitling it *The Grand Coronation Procession of Napoleone, the 1st Emperor of France* (1805). No one called him to pick up a Legion of Honour for returning good taste to France.

The drawing showed a preening, swollen, strutting emperor

Jacques-Louis David, Le Sacre de Joséphine, *1807*

leading a group of flunkeys, flatterers and prisoners. Pope Pius VII was there but, unlike in David's version, Gillray's pope was sheltering in his robes a choirboy, who is taking off his mask to reveal the face of the devil. Josephine, far from the fresh-faced damsel painted by David, was an acne-scarred balloon. Carrying the train of the emperor were representatives of the countries that Napoleon had conquered: Prussia, Spain and Holland. They appeared not to be doing so of their own accord. Behind them were rows of shackled soldiers; this was not an emperor to whom the people had given power willingly. And keeping them in line was the police chief, Joseph Fouché, as Gillray explained in a caption, 'bearing the sword of justice'. It was coated in blood.

Napoleon was furious. He asked Fouché to imprison without trial anyone caught bringing copies of the drawing into France. He made formal diplomatic complaints against Gillray through his ambassador in London and vowed that if he ever succeeded in invading England, he would come looking for the artist. The reaction was characteristic. When negotiating the Treaty of Amiens with England in 1802, Napoleon had even attempted to insert a clause stating that all caricaturists who drew him should be treated like murderers or forgers and be extradited to stand trial in France. The English negotiators, puzzled, turned down the request.

2

Louis-Philippe and Napoleon would not have responded in such a way if humour were just a game. As they were the first to recognize, jokes are a way of anchoring a criticism. They are another way of complaining: about arrogance, cruelty or pomposity, about departures from virtue and good sense.

If they are a particularly effective way of complaining, it is because they communicate a lesson while seeming only to entertain us. Comics have no need to deliver a sermon outlining abuses of power. They lead us to acknowledge in a chuckle the aptness of their complaints against authority.

Furthermore (the prison sentences of Philipon notwithstanding), the apparent innocence of jokes allows comics to convey messages that could be dangerous or impossible to voice directly. Historically, it is the jesters at court who have been allowed to tell royals serious things that could not have been said to them seriously (when King James I of England, who presided over a notoriously corrupt clergy, had trouble fattening up one of his horses, Archibald Armstrong, the court fool, was said to have told him that he had only to make the horse into a bishop for the creature rapidly to put on the

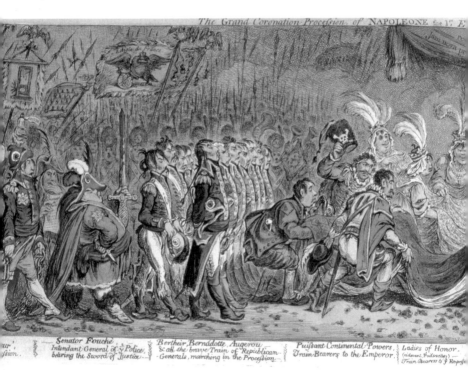

necessary pounds). In his *The Joke and Its Relation to the Unconscious* (1905), Freud wrote, 'A joke will allow us to exploit something ridiculous in our enemy which we could not, on account of obstacles in the way, bring forward openly or consciously.' Through jokes, Freud continued, critical messages 'can gain a reception with the hearer which they would never have found in a non-joking form . . . [which is why] jokes are especially favoured in order to make criticism possible against persons in exalted positions'.

That said, not every exalted person is ripe for comic treatment. We rarely laugh at a doctor performing an important surgical operation. Yet we may laugh at a doctor who, after an operation, returns home and intimidates his wife and daughters by talking

James Gillray, The Grand Coronation Procession of Napoleone, the 1st Emperor of France, *1805*

to them in pompous medical jargon. We laugh at what is unwarranted and disproportionate. We laugh at kings whose self-image has outgrown their worth, whose goodness has not kept up with their power. We laugh at high-status individuals who have forgotten their humanity and are abusing their privileges. We laugh at, and through our laughter criticize, evidence of injustice and excess.

In the hands of the best comics, laughter hence acquires a moral purpose, jokes become attempts to cajole others into reforming their characters and habits. Jokes are a way of sketching a political ideal, of creating a more equitable and saner world. As Samuel Johnson saw it, satire is only another way, and a particularly effective one, of 'censuring wickedness or folly'. In the words of John Dryden, 'the true end of satire is the amendment of vices'.

3

History reveals no shortage of jokes attempting to amend the vices of high-status groups, to shake the mighty from pretension or dishonesty.

In late eighteenth-century England it became fashionable for wealthy young women to wear colossal wigs. Cartoonists offended by the absurdity of the trend quickly produced drawings that amounted to a safe way of telling these women to come to their senses – a message that, as Freud recognized, would have been hard for a cartoonist to convey directly when the objects of his criticism owned large tracts of the realm.

At the same time, a fashion for breastfeeding set in among high-society women, who had never concerned themselves with babies before, but began to suckle to fit in with progressive ideas on motherhood. Women who hardly knew where the nursery was

Engraving from the Oxford *magazine, 1771*

James Gillray, The Fashionable Mamma, *1796*

insisted on exposing their breasts, often between courses at lunches and dinners. Once again, the cartoonists stepped in to call for moderation.

By the second half of the nineteenth century, another affected habit had taken root among the upper classes of England: a vogue for speaking French, especially in restaurants, to indicate seriousness and eminence. *Punch* sensed the presence of a fresh vice to amend.

SCENE - *A Restaurant near Leicester Square.*

Jones. "OH - ER - GARSONG, REGARDEZ EECEE - ER - APPORTEZ - VOO LE - LA - "
Waiter. "BEG PARDON, SIR. I DON'T KNOW FRENCH!"
Jones. "THEN FOR GOODNESS' SAKE, SEND ME SOMEBODY WHO *DOES!* "

Punch, *1895*

In the United States, a century later, there was still plenty of 'wickedness and folly' at large among Manhattan's elite for the cartoonists of the *New Yorker* to focus on. In business, many chief executives had acquired an interest in seeming friendly to their employees. Unfortunately, their interest stopped short of a willingness actually to be so. They merely contented themselves with camouflaging many of their more brutal practices in bland technocratic language – which, they hoped, might lend respectability to exploitation not very different from that of the satanic mills of old. The cartoonists were not fooled.

Slave galley: 'Human resources?'

Businesses remained committed to a starkly utilitarian view of their employees – in which genuine, rather than ritualistic, talk of these employees' fulfilment, or of the responsibilities of an organization to them, was tantamount to a heresy.

'You know what I think folks? What's
important is to be warm, decent human beings ...'

Such were the demands of business that many high-ranking executives, especially lawyers, allowed the clinically efficient mindset of their jobs to permeate all areas of their lives, at the expense of spontaneity or sympathy.

'I consider myself a passionate man, but a lawyer first.'

*'Joyce, I'm so madly in love with you,
I can't eat, etc. but that's not why I called …'*

Meanwhile, a military class enjoyed unparalleled prestige based on the power to destroy the globe. The comics encouraged their audience to smile critically at the deathly serious demeanour of the generals.

4

Not only is humour a useful tool with which to attack high-status others, it may also help us to make sense of and moderate our own status anxieties.

Much that we find funny focuses on situations or feelings that in ordinary life we would be liable to encounter with embarrassment or shame. The greatest comics place their fingers on vulnerabilities that we cannot examine in the light of day; they pull us from our lonely relationship with our most awkward sides. The more private and intense the worry, the greater the possibility of laughter, laughter being a tribute to the skill with which the unmentionable has been skewered.

Unsurprisingly, therefore, much humour reveals an attempt to name, and thereby contain, anxiety about status. It reassures us that there are others in the world no less envious or socially fragile than we are; that there are fellow spirits waking up in the early hours tormented by their financial performance; and that beneath the sober appearance society demands of us, most of us are going a little out of our minds – giving us cause to hold out a hand to our comparably tortured neighbours.

'Which Microsoft Millionaire are you thinking about now?'

*'I usually wake up screaming at six-thirty,
and I'm in the office by nine.'*

Rather than *mocking* us for our concern with status, the kindest comics *tease* us: they criticize us while implying that we remain essentially acceptable. Thanks to their skills, we acknowledge with an open-hearted laugh bitter truths about ourselves that we might have recoiled from in anger or hurt had they been levelled at us in an ordinary, accusatory way.

5

Comics, no less than other artists, hence slip rewardingly into Matthew Arnold's definition of art as a discipline offering criticism of life. Their work strives to amend both the injustices of power and the excesses of our envy towards those higher in the social system. Like tragedy it is motivated by some of what is most regrettable about our condition.

The underlying, unconscious aim of comics may be to bring about – through the adroit use of humour – a world in which there will be a few less things to laugh about.

'Of course they're clever. They have to be clever. They haven't got any money.'

III.
POLITICS

Ideal Human Types

1

Every society holds certain kinds of people in high esteem – while condemning or ignoring others, for having the wrong skills, accent, temperament, gender or skin colour. Yet these definitions of success are far from permanent or universal. Qualities and skills that would result in high status in one place have a marked tendency to grow irrelevant or be frowned upon in another.

To sink a shaft into selected strata of history reveals a catholic range of what different societies in different ages have chosen to view as an honourable person.

Requirements of High Status in:

Sparta, Greek peninsula, 400 BC

The most honoured members of ancient Spartan society were men and in particular fighting, aggressive men with large muscles, a vigorous (bi)sexual appetite, little interest in family life, a distaste for business and luxury, and an enthusiasm for killing, especially Athenians, on the battlefield. The fighters of Sparta never used money, they avoided hairdressers and entertainers, and were unsentimental about wives and children. It was a disgrace for them ever to be seen in the market place. Even knowing how to count was frowned upon for indicating a commercial spirit. From the age of seven, every male Spartan trained to become a soldier, lived and ate in barracks, and practised battle manoeuvres. Even when married, men did not share a home with their wives, though they were allowed to spend one night a month with them in order to perpetuate themselves. If any children were born weak, it was common practice for them to be taken out to the barren slopes of Mount Taygetus and left to die.

Western Europe, AD 476–1096

Following the collapse of the Roman Empire in the West, in many parts of Europe the most revered individuals became those who modelled themselves on the life and teachings of Jesus Christ. Saints, as the Church deemed them, never took up arms, never killed other human beings and tried to avoid killing animals as well (like many saints, St Bernard was a vegetarian and was said to have walked very slowly, with his eyes on the ground, in order to avoid stepping on ants, God's creatures too). Saints shunned material goods. They didn't own houses or horses. St Hilarion lived in a cell 5 foot by 4 foot. St Francis of Assisi claimed that he was married to 'Lady Poverty', while he and his followers lived in wattle and daub huts, had no tables or chairs and slept on the floor. St Anthony of Padua ate only roots and grasses. St Dominic de Guzman averted his eyes when he passed the houses of rich merchants. Saints tried to suppress sexual feelings and were noted for their extreme physical modesty. St Casimir turned away a virgin placed in his bed by his family. St Thomas Aquinas was said to have been locked up in a tower with a woman who used her beauty and perfumes to seduce him, but though he was momentarily aroused, he thrust her away and accepted from God 'a girdle of perpetual virginity'.

Western Europe, c. 1096–1500

In the period after the First Crusade, it was the turn of knights to become the most admired people in Western European society. Knights came from wealthy families, they lived in castles, they slept in beds, they ate meat and they approved of killing people they thought un-Christian (especially Muslims). When they were not killing people, they turned their attention to animals. John de Grailly was said to have killed 4,000 wild boars. Knights were accomplished lovers too and wooed women at court, often through the skilful use of poetry. They especially prized virgins. They were interested in money, but only when it came from land, not trade. They also liked horses. 'Knights have not been chosen to ride an ass or a mule,' reported Gutierre Diaz de Gamez (1379–1450), author of *The Unconquered Knight* (*c.* 1431). 'Knights do not come from among feeble or timid or cowardly souls, but from among men who are strong and full of energy, bold and without fear, and for this reason there is no other beast that so befits a knight as a good horse.'

England, 1750–1890

In England by 1750 it was no longer judged necessary to know how to fight in order to be respectable. Dancing was more important. The most admired people in society were 'gentlemen'. They were wealthy, they tended not to do very much apart from presiding over the management of their estates, they dabbled in industry or trade (especially with India and the West Indies), but they were keen to distinguish themselves from the inferior caste of merchants and industrialists. They were supposed to like their families and avoid placing their children on hillsides for them to die – and yet they could keep a mistress in town.

Emphasis was placed on perfecting a languid elegance. It was important to take care of one's hair and visit a barber regularly. Lord Chesterfield, in his *Letters to His Son* (1751), advised that a gentleman's conversation should be free from 'misplaced eagerness' that could result in the use of 'trifling or ill-timed anecdotes with silly preambles like "I will tell you an excellent thing"'. Chesterfield also stressed that gentlemen should know how to dance a minuet: 'Remember that the graceful motion of the arms, the giving of your hand, and the putting-on and putting-off of your hat genteelly are the material parts of a gentleman's dancing.' As for relations with women, a gentleman was meant to marry, while bearing in mind that (in Chesterfield's words) 'women are only children of a larger growth'. If seated next to an example at dinner, a gentleman was to 'prattle' on to her rather than be silent, which she might mistake for dullness or arrogance.

Brazil, 1600–1960

Among the Cubeo tribe of the north-west Amazon, individuals with the highest status were men who spoke very little (one's strength was supposed to seep out if one babbled), did not partake in dances, did not involve themselves in raising children but were, first and foremost, skilled at killing jaguars. Whereas low-status men were relegated to fishing, high-status ones went hunting. A person who killed a jaguar would wear its teeth on a necklace. The more jaguars one killed, the more chance one had of becoming the 'headman' or tribal chief. Headmen wore large jaguar-tooth necklaces as well as an armadillo girdle. Women were condemned to cultivating the manioc root in jungle clearings. Few things brought more shame upon a man than for him to be found helping his wife prepare a root-based meal.

2

What are the principles by which status is distributed? Why are military men applauded in one society, landed gentlemen in another?

At least four answers suggest themselves. A group may acquire status by being able to harm others physically, bullying and threatening a population to offer its respect.

Or it may win status by being able to defend others, through strength, patronage or the command of foodstuffs. When safety is in short supply (ancient Sparta, Europe in the twelfth century), courageous fighters and knights on horseback will be celebrated.

When a community craves nutrients only available from elusive animal flesh (the Amazon), it is the killers of jaguars who will earn respect and its symbol, the armadillo girdle. In countries where the livelihood of the majority depends on trade and high technology, entrepreneurs and scientists will be the targets of admiration (modern Europe and North America). The converse also holds true: a group which cannot provide a service to others will end up without status – the fate of muscular men in societies with secure borders or jaguar hunters in settled agricultural societies.

Or a group may acquire elevated status by impressing others with its goodness, its physical talents, its artistic skills or its wisdom – as in the case, for example, of saints in Christian Europe, and footballers in modern Europe.

Or a group may appeal to the conscience or sense of moral decency of its fellow inhabitants, so eloquently articulating the justice of its cause that no one seeking to retain a good self-image will remain deaf to its calls for a redistribution of status.

As the determinants of high status keep altering, so too, naturally, will the triggers of status anxiety. In one group we may worry about our capacity to launch a spear into the flank of an animal, in another about our strength on the battlefield, in a third about our capacity for devotion to God, and in a fourth about our ability to wrest a profit from the capital markets.

3

For those left most anxious or embittered by the ideals of their own societies, the history of status, even when crudely sketched, cannot but reveal a basic and inspiring point: that ideals are not cast of stone. Status ideals have long been, and may again in the future be, subject to alteration. And the word we might use to describe this process of change is politics.

Through political battles, different groups will attempt to shape the honour system of their communities in order to win dignity for themselves in the face of opposition from those with a stake in a prior arrangement. Through a ballot box, a gun, a strike or some-times a book, these different groups will strive to redirect their community's notions of who is rightfully owed the privileges of a high-status position.

A Political Perspective on Modern Status Anxiety

1

If the capacity to hunt jaguars, dance a minuet, ride a horse in battle or imitate the life of Christ no longer offers sufficient grounds to be labelled a success, what, then, might be said to constitute the dominant contemporary Western ideal according to which people are judged and status allotted?

One might, without making scientific claims for the portrait, sketch at least some of the concerns and qualities of the prototypical modern successful person, the inheritor of the high status once claimed by the warrior, the saint, the knight or the aristocratic landed gentleman.

Requirements of High Status in:

London, New York, Los Angeles, Sydney, 2004

The category of the successful person comprises both men and women, of any race, who have been able to accumulate money, power and renown through their own activities (rather than through inheritance) in one of the myriad branches of the commercial world (including sport, art and scientific research). Because societies are practically trusted to be 'meritocratic', financial achievements are understood to be 'deserved'. The ability to accumulate wealth is prized for reflecting the presence of at least four cardinal virtues: creativity, courage, intelligence and stamina. The presence of other virtues – humility or godliness, for example – rarely detains attention. Achievements are not attributed, as in past societies, to 'luck', 'providence' or 'God' – a reflection of modern secular societies' faith in individual willpower. Financial failures are, correspondingly, judged to be merited, with unemployment bearing some of the shame of physical cowardice in warrior eras. Money is imbued with an ethical quality. Its presence indicates the virtue of its owner, as do the material goods it can buy. Like jaguar teeth for the Cubeo, a prosperous way of life signals worthiness, while the ownership of an ancient car or threadbare home may spark suppositions of moral deficiency. Aside from offering high status, wealth is promoted on the basis of its capacity to deliver happiness, through access to a range of ever-changing consumer goods – whose absence may fill us with pity and wonder when we consider the restricted lives of previous generations.

2

However natural such a status-ideal may appear, it is, of course – a political perspective alerts us – only the work of humans; a recent development dating back to the middle of the eighteenth century, brought into being by a host of identifiable factors. Furthermore, the political perspective would add, the ideal is occasionally simple-minded, at times unfair and perhaps not wholly unchangeable.

No aspect of the modern ideal has come under greater scrutiny than the association it constructs between wealth and virtue – and poverty and dubiousness. In *The Theory of the Leisure Class* (1899), Thorstein Veblen described how money had in the early nineteenth century emerged as the central criterion in shaping the way commercial societies evaluated their members: '[Wealth has become] the conventional basis of esteem. Its possession has become necessary in order to have any reputable standing in the community. It has become indispensable to acquire property in order to retain one's good name ... Those members of the community who fall short of [a relatively high standard of wealth] will suffer in the esteem of their fellow men; and consequently they will suffer also in their own esteem.'

In a commercial society, it would, Veblen implied, be almost impossible to hold on to the thought that one was virtuous and *yet* poor. The most unmaterialistically minded person would sense an imperative to accumulate wealth and demonstrate possession of it to escape opprobrium, and would feel anxious and to blame as a result of a failure to do so.

Accordingly, the possession of a great many material goods becomes necessary not principally because these goods yield pleasure (though they may do this too), but because they confer honour. In the ancient world, a debate had raged among philosophers about what was materially necessary for happiness and what unnecessary. Epicurus, for one, had argued that simple food and shelter were necessary, but expensive houses and luxurious dishes could safely be bypassed by all rational, philosophically minded people. However, reviewing the argument many centuries later in *The Wealth of Nations*, Adam Smith wryly pointed out that in modern, materialistic societies there were no doubt countless things which were unnecessary from the point of view of physical survival, but at the same time a great many more things had, practically speaking, come to be counted as 'necessaries', because no one could be thought respectable and so lead a psychologically comfortable life without owning them:

'By necessaries I understand not only the commodities which are indispensably necessary for the support of life, but whatever the custom of the country renders it indecent for creditable people, even of the lowest order, to be without. A linen shirt, for example, is, strictly speaking, not a necessary of life. The Greeks and Romans lived, I suppose, very comfortably though they had no linen. But in the present times, through the greater part of Europe, a creditable day-labourer would be ashamed to appear in public without a linen shirt, the want of which would be supposed to denote that disgraceful degree of poverty which, it is presumed, nobody can well fall into without extreme bad conduct. Under necessaries, therefore, I comprehend not only those things which nature, but those things which the established rules of decency have rendered necessary to the lowest rank of people.'

Since Smith's day, economists have been almost unanimous in subscribing to the idea that what defines, and lends bitterness to, the state of poverty is not so much direct physical suffering as the shame that flows from the negative reactions of others to one's state, from the way that poverty flouts what Smith termed 'the established rules of decency'. In *The Affluent Society* (1958), J. K. Galbraith proposed, with a bow to Smith, 'People are poverty-stricken whenever their income, even if adequate for survival, falls markedly behind that of the community. Then they cannot have what the larger community regards as the minimum necessary for decency; and they cannot wholly escape, therefore, the judgement of the larger community that they are indecent.'

3

It is this idea that 'decency' should be attached to wealth – and 'indecency' to poverty – that forms the core of one strand of sceptical complaint against the modern status-ideal. Why should a failure to make money be taken as a sign of an unconditionally flawed human being rather than of a fiasco in one particular area of the far larger, more multifaceted, project of leading a good life? Why should both wealth and poverty be read as the predominant guides to an individual's morals?

The reasons are not mysterious. To earn money frequently calls upon virtues of character. To hold down almost any job requires intelligence, energy, forethought and the ability to cooperate with others. Indeed, the more lucrative the job, the greater the merits it may demand. Lawyers and surgeons not only earn higher salaries than street cleaners, their occupations typically involve more sustained effort and skill.

A day-labourer would be ashamed to appear in public without a linen shirt, wrote Adam Smith, because (to return to his passage with italics) not having such a shirt would imply a degree of poverty which, Smith's contemporaries presumed, '*nobody can well fall into without extreme bad conduct*'. Only if a man was a congenital drunk, unreliable, thieving or childishly insubordinate would he be refused the modest employment that buying a linen shirt requires – in which case, one can appreciate how the ownership of a shirt might safely be taken as a minimum guarantee of good character.

It is a short step from here to go on to imagine that *extreme good conduct* and many virtues must lie behind the acquisition of cupboards full of linen shirts, and yachts, mansions and jewels. The notion of a status symbol, a costly material object that confers respect upon its owner, rests upon the widespread and not improbable idea that the acquisition of the most expensive goods must inevitably demand the greatest of all qualities of character.

4

However, opponents of an economic meritocracy have long argued that true merit must be a more elusive, complex quality than anything that could neatly be captured by the parameters of an end-of-year salary – a scepticism analogous to that of certain educationalists who will deny that the 'intelligence' of a group of students can ever be measured properly by making them sit an examination and grading them according to their answers to questions like:

Pick out the antonyms from among these four words:

obdurate   spurious   ductile   recondite

Which is not a way for these critics to argue that merit or intelligence is equally distributed or indeed immeasurable, but simply to insist that you or I are unlikely ever to know how to do the measuring properly and hence should display infinite care before acting in ways that presume we can; for example, in the economic sphere, by abolishing taxes for the wealthy (who, it is occasionally said by extreme defenders of economic meritocracy, deserve to maintain all their earnings) or removing state benefits (so that the poor, these same defenders would add, can more fully experience the depths of the deprivation they too must deserve).

Such scepticism does not sit easily with the demands of everyday life. It is easy to understand the wish for a system, be it educational or economic, that assures us that we can pick out the worthy candidates from a classroom or society and, in turn, can walk past the suffering of the losers *with good conscience.*

However, an urgent wish is no guarantee of a sound solution. In *The Intelligent Woman's Guide to Socialism and Capitalism* (1928), George Bernard Shaw argued that modern capitalist societies had fallen prey to a particularly obtuse system of determining a hierarchy: they had settled for a system operating under the belief that, 'If every man is left to make as much money as he can for himself in his own way, subject only to the laws restraining crude violence and direct fraud, then wealth will spontaneously distribute itself in proportion to the industry, sobriety and generally the virtue of the citizens, the good men becoming rich and the bad men poor.'

But in fact, continued Shaw, it is clear that any ruthless, ambitious man 'can grab three or four million pounds for himself by selling bad whiskey or by forestalling the wheat harvest and selling it at three times its cost or by running silly newspapers and magazines that circulate deceitful advertisements', while 'men who exercise their noble faculties or risk their lives in the furtherance of human knowledge and welfare' can end up in poverty and insignificance.

That said, Shaw did not wish to align himself with sentimental voices who might claim that, under the current arrangement of society, god men always became poor – a piece of reasoning no less simplistic than the opposite. Rather, he sought to imbue us with a sense of the limitations of judging anyone morally on the basis of salary; and an attendant desire to soften the many consequences that might flow from differences in wealth.

In *Unto This Last* (1862), John Ruskin, who had been as concerned with challenging meritocratic ideas, described in sarcastic tones the conclusions he had reached about the characters of rich and poor on the basis of hundreds of encounters with both groups in many countries over four decades: 'The persons who become rich are, generally speaking, industrious, resolute, proud, covetous, prompt, methodical, sensible, unimaginative, insensitive and ignorant. The persons who remain poor are the entirely foolish, the entirely wise, the idle, the reckless, the humble, the thoughtful, the dull, the imaginative, the sensitive, the well-informed, the improvident, the irregularly and impulsively wicked, the clumsy knave, the open thief and the entirely merciful just and godly person.'

In other words, an unclassifiably wide range of people ends up both rich and poor – which means, to follow the message first articulated by Jesus Christ and repeated in secular language by political thinkers across the nineteenth and twentieth centuries, that it is not our prerogative to start to ascribe honour principally on the basis of income. A multitude of outer events and inner characteristics will go into making one man wealthy and another destitute. There are luck and circumstance, illness and fear, accident and late development, good timing and misfortune.

Three centuries before Ruskin and Shaw, Michel de Montaigne had in a similar vein stressed the role of contingent factors in determining the outcome of lives. He had advised us to remember the role played by 'chance in bestowing glory on us according to her fickle will: I have often seen chance marching ahead of merit, and often outstripping merit by a long chalk'. A dispassionate audit of our successes and failures should leave us feeling that there are reasons at once to be less proud of and less embarrassed by ourselves, for a thought-provoking percentage of what happens to us is not of our own doing. Montaigne asked that we keep a rein on our excitement when meeting the powerful and wealthy and on our judgements when encountering the poor and obscure. 'A man may have a great suite of attendants, a beautiful palace, great influence and a large income. All that may *surround* him, but it is not *in* him ... Measure his height with his stilts off: let him lay aside his wealth and his decorations and show himself to us naked ... What sort of soul does he have? Is his soul a beautiful one, able, happily endowed with all her functions? Are her riches her own or are they borrowed? Has luck had nothing to do with it? ... That is what we need to know; that is what the immense distances between us men should be judged by.'

Uniting the many challenges to the commercial meritocratic ideal is a plea that we cease bestowing something as haphazardly distributed as money may have been with moral connotations; that we cut the doctrinaire connections routinely made between wealth and virtue – and that we attempt to ensure that we have taken the stilts off before we begin to judge.

5

Aside from the connection it posits between making money and being good, the modern ideal of a successful life imputes a further connection: between making money and being happy.

This idea in turn rests on three assumptions. First, that to identify what will make us happy is not an inordinately difficult task. Just as our bodies typically know what they need in order to be healthy and hence direct us towards smoked fish when they lack sodium or peaches when blood sugar is low, so too, the theory goes, our minds can be relied upon to understand what we should aim for in order to flourish; and so they will naturally push us towards certain careers and projects. Second, that the enormous range of occupational possibilities and consumer goods available in modern civilization is not a gaudy, enervating show responsible for stoking up desires with little relevance to our welfare but rather is capable of satisfying some of our most important needs. And, third, that the more money we have available to us, the more products and services we will be able to afford, and so the greater our chances of happiness will be.

The most suggestive and readable adversary of this group of assumptions remains Jean-Jacques Rousseau and his *Discourse on the Origin of Inequality*. Rousseau began by claiming that, however independent-minded we might judge ourselves to be, we are dangerously poor at understanding our own needs. Our souls rarely articulate what they must have in order to be satisfied, or, when they do mumble something, their commands are likely to be misfounded or contradictory. Rather than comparing the mind with a body correct in its sense of what it should consume in order to be healthy, Rousseau invited us to think of it as being more like a body that cries out for wine when it needs water and insists it should be dancing when it should in truth be flat on a bed. Our minds are susceptible to the influence of external voices telling us what we require to be satisfied, voices that may drown out the faint sounds emitted by our souls and can distract us from the careful, arduous task of correctly tracing our priorities.

Rousseau went on to sketch the history of the world not as a story of progress from barbarism to the great workshops and cities of Europe, but as one of regress away from a privileged state in which we lived simply but had the chance to sound out our needs, towards one where we were apt to feel envy for ways of life with few connections to our own characters. In technologically backward pre-history, in Rousseau's state of nature, when men and women lived in forests and had never entered a shop or read a newspaper, the philosopher pictured people more easily understanding themselves, and so being drawn towards essential features of a satisfied life: a love of family, a respect for nature, an awe at the beauty of the universe, a curiosity about others, and a taste for music and simple entertainments. It was from this state that modern commercial 'civilization' had pulled us, leaving us to envy and yearn and suffer in a world of plenty.

For those who might interpret this as an absurdly romantic story to be explained away as the fancy of a pastoral author unreasonably angered by modernity, it is worth adding that, if the eighteenth century listened to Rousseau's argument, it was in part because it had before it one stark example of its apparent truths in the shape of the fate of the native populations of North America.

Reports of American Indian society drawn up in the sixteenth century had described it as materially simple, but psychologically rewarding: communities were small, close-knit, egalitarian, religious, playful and martial. The Indians were certainly backward in a financial sense. They lived off fruits and wild animals, they slept in tents, they had few possessions. Every year, they wore the same pelts and shoes. Even a chief might own no more than a spear and a few pots. But there was reputed to be an impressive level of contentment amidst the simplicity.

However, within only a few decades of the arrival of the first Europeans, the status system of Indian society was revolutionized through contact with the technology and luxury of European industry. What mattered was no longer one's wisdom or understanding of the ways of nature, but one's ownership of weapons, jewellery and alcohol. Indians now longed for silver earrings, copper and brass bracelets, tin finger rings, necklaces made of Venetian glass, ice chisels, guns, alcohol, kettles, beads, hoes and mirrors.

These new enthusiasms did not come about by coincidence. European traders deliberately attempted to foster desires in the

Indians, so as to motivate them to hunt the animal pelts that the European market required. By 1690, the English naturalist the Reverend John Banister was reporting that the Indians of the Hudson Bay area had been successfully tempted by traders to want 'many things which they had not wanted before, because they never had them, but which by means of trade are now highly necessary to them'. Two decades later, the traveller Robert Beverley observed, 'The Europeans have introduced luxury among the Indians which has multiplied their wants and made them desire a thousand things they never even dreamt of before.'

Unfortunately, these thousand things, however ardently sought, didn't appear to make the Indians much happier. Certainly they worked harder. Between 1739 and 1759, the 2,000 warriors of the Cherokee tribe were estimated to have killed 1.25 million deer to satisfy European demand. In the same period, the Montagnais Indians on the north shore of the St Lawrence river traded between 12,000 and 15,000 pelts a year with French and British merchants in Tadoussac. But happiness did not increase in line with levels of trade. Rates of suicide and alcoholism rose, communities fractured, factions squabbled among themselves over the European booty. The tribal chiefs didn't need Rousseau to understand what had happened, but they unknowingly concurred with his analysis nevertheless. There were calls for Indians to rid themselves of dependence on European 'luxury'. In the 1760s, the Delawares of western Pennsylvania and the Ohio valley tried to revive the ways of their forefathers. Prophecies were heard that the tribes would be wiped out if they did not wean themselves from dependence on trade. But it was too late. The Indians, no different in their psychological make-up from other humans, succumbed to the easy lures of the trinkets of modern civilization and ceased listening to the quiet voices that spoke of the modest pleasures of the community and of the beauty of the empty canyons at dusk.

6

Defenders of commercial society have always had one answer to American Indian sympathizers, and anyone else who might complain of the corrupting effects of an advanced economy: that no one *forced* the Indians to buy necklaces made of Venetian glass, ice chisels, guns, kettles, beads, hoes and mirrors. No one stopped them living in tents and made them aspire to owning wooden houses with porches and wine cellars. The Indians left behind a sober, simple life of their own accord – which might indicate that this life was perhaps not as pleasant as has been made out.

This defence is similar to that used by modern advertising agents and newspaper editors, who will assert that they are not the ones responsible for encouraging undue concern with the lives of the famous, with changes in fashion or the ownership of new products. It is simply that certain branches of the media lay out information related to these topics for anyone who might be interested – while, the implication goes, many more people will spontaneously prefer to help the needy, examine their souls, read Edward Gibbon's *Decline and Fall* or reflect upon the short passage of time before their own extinction.

This response illuminates why Rousseau wished to place so much emphasis, unedifying though it might have been, on the difficulty humans have in making up their own minds about what is important, their predisposition to listen to other people's suggestions about where their thoughts should be directed and what they should value in order to be happy, particularly when the suggestions are accompanied by the authority of a newspaper or the visual charms of a billboard.

It is ironic that it should be advertising agents and newspaper editors themselves who are typically the first to downplay the effectiveness of their own trades. They will insist that the population is independently minded enough not to be overly affected by the stories which they themselves lay before the world, or to be taken in for long by the siren calls of billboards they have themselves so artfully designed.

They are, unfortunately, being too modest. Nothing more sharply illustrates the extent of their disingenuousness than reports of the rapid way in which what was once a possibility will, with sufficient prompting, come to seem a necessity.

PERCENTAGE OF NORTH AMERICANS DECLARING THE FOLLOWING ITEMS TO BE NECESSITIES

	1970	2000
Second car	20 %	59 %
Second television	3 %	45 %
More than one telephone	2 %	78 %
Car air-conditioning	11 %	65 %
Home air-conditioning	22 %	70 %
Dishwasher	8 %	44 %

Criticisms of consumer society have focused not only on the shortcomings and inadequacies of products (a point easy to exaggerate, for it takes a curmudgeonly spirit not to appreciate, for example, the beauty of a cashmere pullover or a car's dashboard on a nighttime drive along a motorway), but also, more fairly perhaps, on the distorted picture of our needs that ensues from the way these products are presented to us. They can appear essential, blessed with extraordinary powers to bestow happiness on us, because we understand neither their actual identities nor our own functioning.

A car advertisement will, for example, be careful to ignore aspects of our psychology and of the overall process of ownership that could spoil, or at least mitigate, our joy at coming to possess a featured vehicle. It will fail to mention our tendency to cease appreciating anything after owning it a short while. The quickest way to stop

The new SL-Class

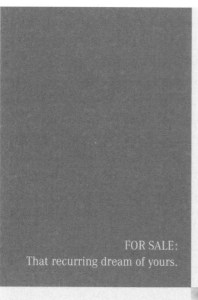

FOR SALE:
That recurring dream of yours.

Mercedes-Benz

noticing something may be to buy it – just as the quickest way to stop appreciating a person may be to marry them. We are tempted to believe that certain achievements and possessions will guarantee us an enduring satisfaction. We are led to imagine ourselves scaling the steep sides of the cliff face of happiness to reach a wide, high plateau on which to continue our lives; we are not reminded that soon after reaching the summit we will be called down again into fresh lowlands of anxiety and desire.

HOW WE IMAGINE SATISFACTION AFTER AN ACQUISITION/ACHIEVEMENT

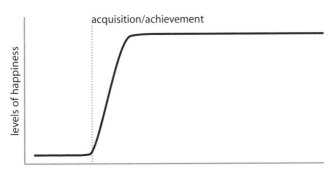

WHAT IN FACT HAPPENS AFTER AN ACQUISITION/ACHIEVEMENT

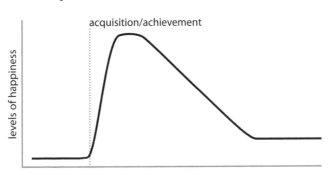

Life seems a process of replacing one anxiety with another and substituting one desire for another – which is not to say that we should never strive to overcome any anxieties or fulfil any desires, but that we should perhaps build into our strivings an awareness of the way our goals promise us levels of rest and resolution that they cannot, by definition, deliver.

The car will quickly be absorbed, like all the wonders we may already own, into the material backdrop of our lives, where it will hardly be noticed – until the night a burglar does us the paradoxical service of breaking a window to steal the radio and reminds us, in the midst of the shattered glass, how much there was to be grateful for.

The advertisement stays quiet too about the weak capacity of all material goods to alter our levels of happiness, as compared with the overwhelming power of emotional events. The most elegant and accomplished of vehicles cannot bring us a fraction of the satisfaction of a relationship – just as it cannot be of any comfort whatever following a domestic argument or abandonment. At such moments, we may even come to resent a car's impassive efficiency, the punctilious clicking of its indicators and the methodical calculations of its onboard computer.

We are equally prone to misunderstand the attractions of certain careers, because so much of what they entail has been edited out, leaving only highlights it would be impossible not to admire. We read of the results, but not the process.

If we cannot stop envying, it is especially poignant that we should spend so much of our lives envying the wrong things.

7

The essence of the charge made against the modern high-status ideal is that it is guilty of a gigantic distortion of priorities, of elevating to the highest level of achievement a process of material accumulation which should be only one of the many things determining the direction of our lives under a more truthful, more broadly defined conception of ourselves.

Incensed by this distortion of priorities, John Ruskin excoriated nineteenth-century Britons (he had never been to the United States) for being the most wealth-obsessed people who had ever emerged in the history of the world. They were, he wrote, at all times, never far from a concern with who had what and from where ('The ruling goddess may be best generally described as the "Goddess of Getting-on"'). They felt shame at their lack of wealth and jealousy at the wealth of others.

But Ruskin made a confession. Contrary to expectations, he too was frantic to become wealthy. The thought of wealth preyed on his mind from breakfast till dinner, he admitted. Yet he was only sarcastically toying with an ambiguity in the word 'wealth' to bring home more forcefully how far he felt his fellow countrymen had strayed from virtue. For the dictionary tells us that wealth means not only, or historically even primarily, large amounts of money. It means an abundance of anything, from butterflies to books to smiles. Ruskin was interested in wealth, he was obsessed by it even. However, it was wealth of an unusual kind that he had in mind: he wished to be wealthy in kindness, curiosity, sensitivity, humility, godliness and intelligence – a set of qualities he referred to simply as 'life'. In *Unto This Last*, he therefore entreated us to set aside our ordinary monetary conceptions of wealth in order to take up a 'life'-based view, according to which the wealthiest people in the land would no longer automatically be the merchants and the landowners, but those who most keenly felt wonder beneath the stars at night or were best able to interpret and alleviate the sufferings of others. 'There is no wealth but life,' he intoned: 'life, including all its powers of love, of joy and of admiration. That country is richest which nourishes the greatest number of noble and happy human beings; that man is richest who, having perfected the functions of his own life to the utmost, has also the widest helpful influence, both personal, and by means of his possessions, over the lives of others . . . Many of the persons commonly considered wealthy are, in reality, no more wealthy than the locks of their own strong boxes, they being inherently and eternally incapable of wealth.'

Ruskin was uttering the plain, childlike truths of the prophets – and, when people did not guffaw (the *Saturday Review* described Ruskin as 'a mad governess' and his thesis as 'windy hysterics', 'absolute nonsense' and 'intolerable twaddle'), they listened. In 1906, Britain's first twenty-seven Labour MPs entered Parliament and were asked what single book had most powerfully influenced them to pursue social justice through politics. Seventeen of them cited Ruskin's *Unto This Last*. Thirteen years later, George Bernard Shaw, in a lecture on the centenary of Ruskin's birth, proposed that the invective of Vladimir Lenin and the indictments of Karl Marx were, when compared with Ruskin's works, like the platitudes of a rural dean (though, because he enjoyed teasing label-fixers, Ruskin had described himself as 'a violent Tory of the old school – Walter Scott's school, that is to say, and Homer's'). 'I have met in my lifetime some extremely revolutionary characters,' Shaw went on, 'and quite a large number of them, when I have asked, "Who put you on to this revolutionary line? Was it Marx?" have answered plainly, "No, it was Ruskin." Ruskinites are perhaps the most thorough-going of all the opponents of the existing state of our society. Ruskin's political message to the cultured people of his day, the class to which he himself belonged, began and ended in this simple judgement: "You are a parcel of thieves."'

Ruskin wasn't alone in the opinion. There were others in the nineteenth century who hammered home, in voices alternately outraged and melancholy, identical criticisms of the way money appeared to have become the chief determinant of respect, something to wield as a sign of demonstrable goodness, and not merely one component, and perhaps not the most important, of a fulfilled life. 'Men are always apt to regard wealth as a precious end in itself and certainly they have never been so apt thus to regard it as they are in England at the present time,' lamented Matthew Arnold in *Culture and Anarchy* (1869). 'Never did people believe anything more firmly, than nine Englishmen out of ten at the present day believe that our greatness and welfare are proved by our being so very rich.' Like Ruskin seven years before him, Arnold urged the subjects of the world's first and most advanced industrial nation to think of wealth as only one of many tools to secure happiness, a quality which he defined in his own way (to further hoots of laughter from critics at the *Daily Telegraph*) as 'an inward spiritual activity, having for its characters increased sweetness, increased light, increased life and increased sympathy'.

Thomas Carlyle agreed, only more angrily. In *Midas* (1843), he asked, 'This successful industry of England, with its plethoric wealth ... which of us has it enriched? ... We have sumptuous garnitures for our life, but have forgotten to *live* in the middle of them. Many men eat finer cookery, drink dearer liquors, but in the heart of them, what increase of blessedness is there? Are they better, beautifuller, stronger, braver? Are they even what they call "happier"? Do they look with satisfaction on more things and human faces in this God's Earth; do more things and human faces look with satisfaction on them? Not so ... We have profoundly forgotten everywhere that cash-payment is not the sole relation of human beings.'

Carlyle was not blind to the benefits of modern enterprise. He even felt the appeal of aspects of accountancy ('book-keeping by double-entry is admirable, and records several things in an exact manner'). But, like Arnold and Ruskin and any number of social critics before and since, he could not accept a way of life in which what he termed 'Mammon-worship' appeared to have subsumed the drive towards 'blessedness' and 'satisfaction' on 'God's Earth'.

Political Change

1

However disgruntled or puzzled a social hierarchy may leave us feeling, we are apt to accept it out of a resigned assumption that it is too entrenched and must be too well founded to be questioned, that communities and the beliefs underpinning them are practically speaking immutable, that they are simply *natural*.

2

Many distinctive ideas have, over the course of history, been thought of as natural:

'Natural' Ideas, 1857–1911

'The real fact is that man in the beginning was ordained to rule over woman: and this is an eternal decree which we have no right and no power to alter.' Earl Percy (1873)

'There is more difference, physically and morally, between an educated European man and a European woman than there is between a European man and a negro belonging to some savage Central African tribe.' Lord Cromer (1911)

'The majority of women (happily for them) are not very much troubled with sexual feeling of any kind.' Sir William Acton (1857)

'As a race the African is inferior to the white man; subordination to the white man is his normal condition. Therefore our system, which

regards the African as an inferior, rests upon a great law of nature.'
Alexander Stephens (1861)

3

A political consciousness could be said to arise through the recognition that views held to be a priori truths by important voices in society may in fact be relative and open to investigation. These views may be declaimed with confidence, they may seem to belong to the fabric of existence as much as the trees and the sky, yet they are – a political perspective insists – made up by particular beings with particular practical and psychological interests to defend.

If this relativity is hard to bear in mind, it is because dominant beliefs typically take pains to suggest that they are no more alterable by human hands than the orbit of the sun. They claim to be merely stating the obvious. They are, to use Karl Marx's helpful word, *ideological*, an ideological statement being defined as one that is engaged in subtly pushing a partial line while pretending to be speaking neutrally.

For Marx, it is the ruling classes of a society who will largely be responsible for disseminating ideological beliefs, which explains why, in societies where a landed class controls the balance of power, the concept of the inherent nobility of landed wealth is taken for granted by the majority of the population (even by many of those who lose out under the system), while in mercantile societies it is the achievements of entrepreneurs which dominate citizens' visions of success. In Marx's phrase, 'The ruling ideas of every age are always the ideas of the ruling class.'

Yet these ideas would never come to rule if they were seen to rule too forcefully. The essence of ideological statements is that, unless our political senses are developed, we will fail to spot them. Ideology is released into society like a colourless, odourless gas. It is embedded in newspapers, advertisements, television programmes and text-books – where it makes light of its partial, perhaps illogical or unjust, take on the world; where it meekly implies that it is simply stating age-old truths with which only a fool or a maniac would disagree.

4

But the nascent political mind casts off politeness and tradition, refuses to blame itself for adopting a contrary stance and asks, with the innocence of a child but the tenacity of a trial lawyer, 'Does this have to be?'

An oppressive situation, which might have been taken as a sign that nature had condemned one to suffer in perpetuity, may – by being reinterpreted politically – be attributed to certain perhaps changeable forces in society. Guilt and shame may be transmuted into understanding and a quest for a more equitable distribution of status.

5

George Bernard Shaw, *The Intelligent Woman's Guide to Socialism and Capitalism* (London, 1928):

'You must clear your mind of the fancy with which we all begin as children, that the institutions under which we live are natural, like the weather. They are not. Because they exist everywhere in our little world, we take it for granted that they have always existed and must always exist. That is a dangerous mistake. They are in fact transient makeshifts. Changes that nobody ever believed possible take place in a few generations. Children nowadays believe that to spend nine years at school, to have old-age and widows' pensions, votes for women and short-skirted ladies in Parliament is part of the order of nature and always was and ever will be; but their great-grandmothers would have said that anyone who told them that such things were coming was mad – and that anyone who wanted them to come was wicked.'

6

The group of people who perhaps most successfully altered their status in Western societies over the twentieth century was women – and the way in which a number of them came to feel entitled to question their positions provides a host of general insights into the development of a political consciousness.

Virginia Woolf began *A Room of One's Own* (1929) by describing a visit she had made one autumn to Cambridge University, during which she had decided to take a look around Trinity College Library – in order to consult the manuscripts of Milton's *Lycidas* and Thackeray's *The History of Henry Esmond*. However, as she was about to step inside the library, 'a deprecating, silvery, kindly gentle-man' had appeared and 'regretted in a low voice that ladies are only admitted to the library if accompanied by a Fellow of the College or furnished with a letter of introduction'. In a minor key, Woolf had come up against one of the great stately pillars upon which the inferior status of women was founded: their disenfranchisement from equal rights to higher education.

Many women would have been hurt by the incident, but few were likely to have responded to the offence politically. Few were likely to have done anything other than blame themselves or nature or God for it. After all, never in history had women had the same rights as men to education. Had not many of the most important doctors in Britain and certain politicians in Parliament too made reference to women's biologically inferior minds, which stemmed from the smaller size of their skulls? What right, then, did any one woman have to doubt the motives of a gentleman who had turned her away from a library, especially if he had delivered his message with apologies and a polite smile?

Woolf was less easily silenced. Performing the quintessential political manoeuvre, rather than asking herself, 'What is wrong with *me* for not being allowed into a library?' she asked, 'What is wrong with *the keepers of the library* for not allowing *me* in?' When ideas and institutions are held to be merely 'natural', responsibility for suffering must necessarily lie either with no one in particular or else with the pained parties themselves. But from a political perspective, we are given leave to imagine that it might be the idea, instead of something in our character, that is at fault. Rather than wondering in disgrace, 'What is wrong with *me* [for being a woman/having dark skin/no money]?', we are encouraged to ask, 'What might be wrong, unjust or illogical about *others* for reproving me?' – a question asked not from any conviction of innocence (the stance of those who use political radicalism as a paranoid way of avoiding self-criticism), but from a recognition that there is more folly and partisanship in institutions, ideas and laws than a naturalistic perspective allows us to imagine.

On her way back to her Cambridge hotel, Woolf therefore moved outwards from her hurt to consider the position of women generally: 'I pondered what effect poverty has on the mind; and what effect wealth has on the mind and I thought how unpleasant it is to be locked out and of the safety and prosperity of the one sex and the poverty and insecurity of the other.' She reflected upon, and felt doubts about, the feminine role-model she had grown up with: of a woman who was always, 'immensely charming and utterly unselfish. She excelled in the difficult arts of family life. She sacrificed herself daily. If there was chicken, she would take the leg; if there was a draught, she would sit in it – in short, she was so constituted that she would never have a mind or a wish of her own, but prefer to sympathize always with the minds and wishes of others.'

On returning to London, the questions continued: 'Why did men drink wine and women water? Why was one sex so prosperous and the other so poor?' Wanting to 'strain off what was personal and accidental in these impressions' of female subjugation, Woolf went to the British Library (into which women had been allowed for the previous two decades) and investigated the history of men's attitudes to women down the ages. She found a stream of extraordinary prejudice and half-baked truth delivered with authority by priests, scientists and philosophers. Women were, it was said, ordained by God to be inferior, they were constitutionally unable to govern or run a business, they were too weak to be doctors, when they had their periods they couldn't be trusted to handle machinery nor to remain impartial during trial cases. And behind this abuse, Woolf recognized that the problem was money. Women didn't have freedom, including freedom of the spirit, because they didn't control their own income: 'Women have always been poor, not for two hundred years merely, but from the beginning of time. Women have had less intellectual freedom than the sons of Athenian slaves.'

Woolf's book culminated in a specific, political demand: women needed not only dignity, but also equal rights to education, an income of 'five hundred pounds a year' and 'a room of one's own'.

7

The ideological element within the modern status-ideal may lack the shrillness of nineteenth-century pronouncements on race or gender. It wears a smile and lies in innocuous places, within the bric-à-brac of what we read and hear. And yet it retains an equally partial and sometimes prejudiced conception of how a good life should be led, which deserves greater scrutiny than it invites.

Messages emanate from society's ubiquitous statements and images to which we are less impermeable than we might think. It

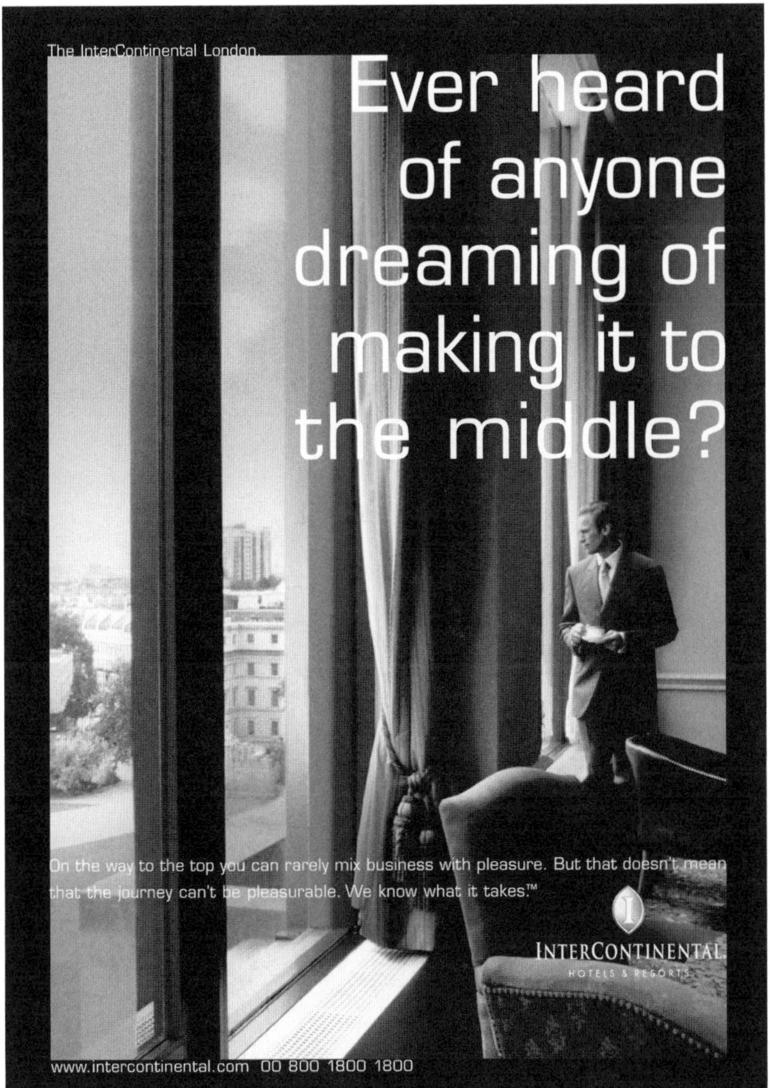
The InterContinental London.
Ever heard of anyone dreaming of making it to the middle?
On the way to the top you can rarely mix business with pleasure. But that doesn't mean that the journey can't be pleasurable. We know what it takes.™
InterContinental
Hotels & Resorts
www.intercontinental.com 00 800 1800 1800

Eddy was determined to escape the mailroom

Ed volunteered for anything he could volunteer for

Edward caught his boss's eye with a shrewd business proposal

Mr. Edward Parks' marketing genius catapulted sales skyward

President E. Parks tells people 'Please, call me Eddy.'

Never settle.

If you're not having breakfast with your client, who is

P.S. We have more first out flights to Europe than any other airline.

It's better to be there **BRITISH AIRWAYS**

would, for example, mean severely underestimating the powers of a Sunday newspaper to trust that we could take in its contents and move on with our sense of priorities and desires no less altered than if we had spent the same period reading a chapter of Jacob Burckhardt's *The Civilization of the Renaissance in Italy* or St Paul's Letter to the Galatians (the ritual of reading the Sunday newspaper having, in the eyes of Max Weber, replaced that of attending church).

8

What the political perspective seeks above all is an understanding of ideology, to reach a point where ideology is denaturalized and defused through analysis – so that we may exchange a puzzled, depressed response to it for a clear-eyed, genealogical grasp of its sources and effects.

When investigated the modern high-status ideal duly ceases to appear natural or God-given. It emerges as a development stemming from changes in industrial production and political organization that began in Britain in the second half of the eighteenth century and subsequently spread across Europe and North America. The enthusiasm for materialism, entrepreneurship and meritocracy infusing newspapers and television schedules ('The ruling ideas of every age are always the ideas of the ruling class') reflects the interests of those at the helm of the system by which the majority earn their living.

Such understanding does not miraculously remove any dis-comforts that might arise from the status-ideal. Understanding bears the same relation to many of the difficulties of politics as a weather satellite does to the crises of meteorology. It cannot always prevent problems, but it can, at a minimum, teach us a host of useful things about the best ways to approach them, sharply diminishing a sense of persecution, passivity and confusion. More ambitiously, understanding may be the first step towards an attempt to shift, or tug at, a society's ideals, helping to bring about a world where it will be marginally less likely that veneration and honour will be dogmatically or unsceptically directed towards those who still have their stilts on.

IV.
CHRISTIANITY

Death

1

The hero of Tolstoy's novella *The Death of Ivan Ilyich* (1886) has long ago fallen out of love with his wife, his children are a mystery to him and he has no friends other than those who can advance him in his career and whose elevated positions will reflect gloriously upon him. Ivan Ilyich is a man overwhelmingly concerned with status. He lives in St Petersburg in a large apartment, decorated according to the fashionable taste of the day, and there gives frequent, soulless dinner parties where nothing of warmth or sincerity is said. He works as a high court judge, enjoying the post chiefly because of the respect it brings him. Sometimes, late at night, Ivan Ilyich reads a book that is 'the talk of the town' and learns from magazines what the correct line to take on it is. Tolstoy sums up the judge's life: 'The pleasures Ivan Ilyich derived from his work were those of pride; the pleasures he derived from society were those of vanity; but it was genuine pleasure that he derived from playing whist.'

Then, at the age of forty-five, Ivan develops a pain in his side which gradually extends across his body. His doctors are at a loss to work out what is wrong. They talk vaguely and pretentiously of floating livers and inharmonious salt levels, and prescribe him a range of ever more expensive and ineffective medicines. He becomes too tired to work, his intestines feel as if they are on fire, he loses his appetite for food and, more significantly, for whist. It slowly dawns upon the judge and on all those around him that he will soon be dead.

This isn't an unpleasant thought for many of Ivan's colleagues in the judiciary. Fyodor Vasilyevich foresees that, with Ivan gone, he will probably get Shtabel's post or Vinnikov's – and that the promotion will mean an increase of 800 roubles plus an allowance for office expenses. Another colleague, Pyotr Ivanovich, works out that there will now be an opportunity to have his brother-in-law transferred from Kaluga, which will please his wife and ease his domestic situation. The news is a little tougher on Ivan's family. His wife, while not directly regretting the death, nevertheless worries about the size of her pension, while his socialite daughter fears that her father's funeral may play havoc with her wedding plans.

For his part, Ivan, with only a few weeks to live, recognizes that he has wasted his time on earth, that he has led an outwardly respectable, but inwardly barren, existence. He looks back at his up-bringing, education and career and finds that everything he did was motivated by the desire to appear important in the eyes of others; his own interests and sensitivities were sacrificed for the sake of impressing people who, he sees only now, do not care a jot for him. One night, in the early hours, tormented by pain, 'it occurred to him that those scarcely perceptible impulses of his to protest at what people of high status considered good, vague impulses which he had always suppressed, might have been precisely what mattered, and all the rest had not been the real thing. His official duties, his manner of life, his family, the values adhered to by people in society and in his profession – all these might not have been the real thing.'

The sense of having wasted his short life is compounded by the recognition that it was only his status that those around him loved, not his true, vulnerable self. He was respected for being a judge, for being a wealthy father and head of household, but with these assets about to disappear, in agony and afraid, he cannot count on anyone's love: 'What tormented Ivan Ilyich most was that no one gave him the kind of compassion he craved. There were moments after long suffering when what he wanted most of all (shameful as it might be for him to admit) was to be pitied like a sick child. He wanted to be caressed, kissed, cried over, as sick children are caressed and comforted. He knew that he was an important functionary with a greying beard, and so this was impossible; yet all the same he longed for it.'

After Ivan has breathed his last, his so-called friends come to pay their respects, but regret all the while the disruption that the death has caused to their whist-playing schedule. Looking at Ivan's waxy, hollow face in its coffin, his colleague Pyotr Ivanovich starts to reflect that death may one day claim him too – and that this could have stern implications, especially for the logic of spending most of his energies on card games. '"Why, the same thing could happen to me at any time now," thought Pyotr Ivanovich and for a moment he felt panic-stricken. But at once, he himself did not know how, he was rescued by the customary reflection that all this had happened to Ivan Ilyich, not to him, that it could not and should not happen to him; and that if he were to grant such a possibility, he would succumb to depression.'

2

The Death of Ivan Ilyich is, in the best tradition of the Christian *memento mori*, a study in how the thought of death may reorient our priorities away from the worldly and towards the spiritual, away from whist and dinner parties towards truth and love.

If Tolstoy understood so well the power of death to change our sense of what we should concern ourselves with, it was because he had himself, only a few years before writing the novella, questioned his own life in the context of a new-found awareness of his mortality. In *A Confession* (1882), a record of his death-inspired interrogations, he explained that, at the age of fifty-one, with *War and Peace* and *Anna Karenina* behind him, world-famous and rich, he had recognized how, from an early age, he had lived not according to his own values, or to those of God, but to those of 'society' and how this had inspired in him a restless desire to be stronger than others; to be more famous, more important and richer than they. In his social circle, 'ambition, love of power, covetousness, lasciviousness, pride, anger and revenge were all respected'. But now, with death in mind, he doubted the validity of his previous ambitions. '"Well, you will have 6,000 desyatinas of land in Samara Government and 300 horses, and what then? ... Very well; you will be more famous than Gogol or Pushkin or Shakespeare or Molière, or than all the writers in the world – and what of it?" I could find no reply at all.'

The answer that eventually quelled his questions was God. He would spend the remainder of his days living in obedience to the teachings of Jesus Christ. Whatever we make of the particularly Christian solution to Tolstoy's crisis of meaning, his sceptical journey follows a familiar trajectory. It is an example of how the thought of death may serve as a guide to a truer, more significant way of life; it is a solemn call, to follow Bach's Cantata BWV 106 (*Gottes Zeit ist die allerbeste Zeit*), to determine our priorities:

Set thy house in order,
For thou shalt die,
And not remain alive.
Bestelle dein Haus,
Denn du wirst sterben,
Und nicht lebendig bleiben.

This is the ancient law:
Man, thou must die.
Yea, come, Lord Jesus.
Es ist der alte Bund:
Mensch, du musst sterben.
Ja, komm, Herr Jesu.

3

But how, in particular, might mortal illness serve to orient us away from an excessive concern with status?

Principally, by removing from us many of the reasons for which society honours its members: for example, the capacity to throw dinner parties, to work effectively and to dispense patronage. In so doing, death reveals the fragility, and so perhaps the worthlessness, of the attentions we stand to gain through status. In good health and at the height of our powers, we are spared an enquiry into whether those who pay us compliments are doing so out of sincere affection or an evanescent search for advantage. We seldom have the courage or cynicism to wonder, 'Is it *me* or *my position in society*?' Yet, by felling the conditions of worldly love, illness renders the distinction quickly and cruelly evident. With death looming, in hospital pyjamas, we are liable to turn in rage against our status-conditional lovers, as angry with ourselves for being vain enough to be seduced by them as with them for orchestrating their heartless seductions. The thought of death brings authenticity to social life. There may be no better way to clear the diary of engagements than to wonder who among our acquaintances would make the trip to the hospital bed.

As conditional love starts to seem less interesting, so too may many of the things we pursue in order to secure it. If wealth, esteem and power buy us the kind of love that will last only so long as our status holds, and yet if we are destined to end our lives defenceless and dishevelled, longing to be comforted like a small child, then we have an unusually clear reason to concentrate our energies on those relationships which will best withstand the erosion of our standing.

4

Herodotus reports that it was the custom towards the end of Egyptian feasts, when revellers were at their most exuberant, for servants to enter banqueting halls and pass between the tables carrying skeletons on stretchers. Regrettably, he does not go on to explain what effect the thought of death was intended to have on the revellers. Would it make them keener to carry on merrymaking or send them home in a new-found spirit of seriousness?

The effect of the thought of death is perhaps to usher us towards whatever happens to matter most to us, be this drinking beside the banks of the Nile, writing a book or making a fortune, and at the same time to encourage us to pay less attention to the verdicts of others, who will not, after all, have to do the dying for us. The prospect of our own extinction may draw us towards the way of life we value in our hearts.

The idea animates Andrew Marvell's renowned attempt to seduce a hesitant young woman into bed through a poem stressing not only her beauty and his fidelity, but also the apparently less romantic fact that she and he will soon enough be no more. With the heroine of 'To His Coy Mistress' (1681) apparently constrained from expressing her desire by anxieties about the views of her peers, Marvell uses the spectre of death to shift her attention away from her status within the community and towards her own wishes. Her coyness would be no crime, explains the poet, if it were not that:

> At my back I always hear
> Time's wingèd charriot hurrying near;
> And yonder all before us lie
> Deserts of vast eternity ...
> The grave's a fine and private place,
> But none, I think, do there embrace.

Shakespeare too seemed aware of the advantages of seducing people by reminding them of their death, a number of his sonnets urge his beloveds to anticipate the moment when:

> Forty winters shall besiege thy brow
> And dig deep trenches in thy beauty's field
> and when time will have changed:
> ... your day of youth to sullied night ...

Though the thought of death may be abused (to panic others into doing what they never wished to do), more hopefully it may help us to correct our tendency to live as if we could afford to defer perpetually our underlying commitments for the sake of propriety. The thought of death may lend us the courage to unhook ourselves from the more gratuitous of society's expectations. Before a skeleton, the repressive aspects of others' opinions have a habit of shedding their powers of intimidation.

5

Whatever differences exist between Christian and secular ideas of the activities which remain meaningful when viewed from the perspective of death, there seems a striking common emphasis on love, on authentic social relations, on charity; and a common condemnation of concerns for power, military strength, financial ambition and glory. There are certain activities that are almost universally unsuited to appear consequential beside the thought of death.

In another passage, Herodotus tells us of Xerxes, mighty King of Persia who, upon successfully invading Greece with an army of nearly 2 million men in 480 BC, at first congratulated himself on his good fortune and abilities as he saw the whole Hellespont filled with the vessels of his fleet and every plain covered with his regiments. But a few moments later he began to weep. His stunned uncle Artabanus, standing beside him, asked him what a man in Xerxes' position could have to cry about. Xerxes replied that he had just realized that in a hundred years' time all those before him, every one of his soldiers and sailors with whose help he had terrified the known world, would be dead.

One might be no less sad, and no less sceptical as to the value of certain achievements and ideas of what is meaningful, when looking at a picture of the participants at a conference for Heinz salesmen in Chicago in the spring of 1902. We might think of the excited plans to raise the volume of ketchup and pickles in stores across the United States – and weep with the bitterness of King Xerxes of Persia.

Heinz salesmen, closing banquet, sales convention, Chicago, 1902

Of course, the erasure of our efforts at the hands of death is apparent in other tasks besides those of conquering nations and building brands. We may look at a mother teaching her dimple-cheeked child to tie his shoelaces and shed as many tears at the thought of both of their eventual funerals. Nevertheless, we may feel that bringing up a child survives the thought of death better than selling condiments; that helping a friend has an edge over leading an army.

'Vanity of vanities, all is vanity,' lamented the author of Ecclesiastes (I.2), 'One generation passeth away, and another generation cometh; but the earth abideth for ever.' And yet, Christian moralists would suggest, not all things are equally vain. In Christian lands, during the sixteenth century, a new subject of art developed and seized the imagination of the art-buying classes for the following two centuries. 'Vanitas art', named in tribute to Ecclesiastes, was hung in domestic environments, often in studies or bedrooms. The canvases featured a table or sideboard on which were arranged a contrasting muddle of objects. There were flowers, coins, a guitar or mandolin, chess games, a laurel wreath and wine bottles: symbols of frivolity and worldly glory. And among these were placed the two great symbols of death and the brevity of life: a skull and an hourglass.

The purpose of these works was not to leave their owners depressed by the vanity of all things. Rather it was to embolden them to find fault with specific aspects of their experience, while at the same time to grant them licence to attend more seriously to the virtues of love, goodness, sincerity, humility and kindness.

Above: *Philippe de Champaigne*, Vanitas, *c. 1671*
Opposite: *Simon Renard de Saint-André*, Vanitas, *c. 1662*

LE TOMBEAV
DES
PLAISIRS
DE I'OVEST
CHAPITRE IV

6

Aside from reflecting on our own mortality, it can also be a relief from status anxiety to dwell on the death of other people, in particular on the death of those whose achievements are now apt to leave us feeling most inadequate and envious. However forgotten and ignored we are, however powerful and revered others may be, we can take comfort from the thought that everyone will ultimately end up as that most democratic of substances: dust.

Outside the village of Walsingham in Norfolk, in 1658, a farmer tilling his field struck upon a row of fifty burial urns, in which a group of aristocrats had been ceremoniously buried in either Roman or Saxon times. The discovery of the urns created a minor sensation in East Anglia and came to the attention of a doctor living in Norwich. By the end of the year, Sir Thomas Browne had used the discovery of the urns as the starting point for a digressive meditation on the futility of striving for worldly greatness, on human imperfectibility and on the related need to recognize our dependence on God for salvation: 'Urne-Buriall, or, A Brief Discourse on the Sepulchrall Urnes lately found in Norfolk'.

'In a field of old Walsingham, not many moneths past, were digged up between fourty and fifty Urnes,' reported Browne in his characteristic cadenced, lumpy English, 'deposited in a dry and sandy soile, not a yard deep, nor farre from one another . . . some containing two pounds of bones, distinguishable in skulls, ribs, jawes, thighbones and teeth.' What interested Browne was how the identity of the dead, at one point the most wealthy and important people of the area, had been entirely lost through time. Some claimed the urns contained Romans, for the burial site was not far from an old Roman garrison; Browne conjectured that they were more likely to be 'our Brittish, Saxon or Danish Forefathers'. Yet no one would ever know their names, let alone in what century they had died. From this, Browne moved on to reflections on the power of time to make a mockery of all our claims to earthly greatness and distinction: 'Who knows the fate of his bones, or how often he is to be buried?' he asked, challenging the dead aristocrats, who might at one time have felt secure of their place in the world, and hosted receptions and played the lyre and looked confidently at themselves in the mirror in the morning. 'There is no antidote against the opium of time ... Generations passe while some trees stand, and old Families last not three Oaks'. In Browne's words, the duty of the honest Christian was to make an impression 'not in the record of man,' rather 'in the Register of God'.

The message might seem a melancholy one, but it is arguably more so for those currently anchoring their lives around the pleasures of a high-status position than for those ignored by society and therefore already well acquainted with the oblivion that their privileged counterparts will eventually be accorded. It is the rich, the beautiful, the famous and the powerful to whom death has the cruellest lessons to teach, the very categories of people whose worldly goods take them, in the Christian understanding, furthest from God.

In England in the middle of the eighteenth century, this Christian-inspired moral was given repeated expression by a group of poets known as the Graveyard School because their staples were poems in which a narrator finds himself in a churchyard on a clear moonlit night and, beside some half-defaced graves, gives way to reflections on the power of death to wipe away achievements and glory – a phenomenon which, it was clear, did not distress the poets overmuch and seemed indeed to be a source of barely suppressed joy. In Edward Young's poem 'Night Thoughts' (1742), the narrator, sitting on a moss-covered gravestone, lets his mind turn to the fate of the great men of the past:

The sage, peer, potentate, king, conqueror
Death humbles these.
Why all this toil for triumphs of an hour?

What though we wade in wealth, or soar in fame?
Earth's highest station ends in 'Here he lies':
And 'Dust to dust' concludes her noblest song.

His contemporary Robert Blair, in 'The Grave' (1743), set in another churchyard, picked up on the same theme:

When self-esteem, or others' adulation,
Would cunningly persuade us we are something
Above the common level of our kind
The grave gainsays the smooth-complexioned flattery
And with blunt truth acquaints us with what we are.

This was a message reiterated by the most distinguished of the Graveyard School, Thomas Gray, in his 'Elegy Written in a Country Churchyard' (1751):

The boast of heraldry, the pomp of power,
And all that beauty, all that wealth e'er gave,
Awaits alike th' inevitable hour.
The paths of glory lead but to the grave.

For those roughly treated by society, there is sweet pre-emptive revenge to be had in anticipating individuals' and society's eventual demise.

Painters too have delighted in producing works depicting their own civilizations in a ruined future form, as a warning to and reprisal against the pompous guardians of the age. So fond was he of painting the great buildings of modern France in ruins that the eighteenth-century French painter Hubert Robert earned himself the nickname 'Robert des Ruines'. In England, his contemporary Joseph Gandy acquired his reputation by painting the Bank of England with the ceiling caved in.

Hubert Robert, Imaginary View of the Grande Gallerie of the Louvre in Ruins, *1796*

Joseph Gandy, View of the Rotunda of the Bank of England in Ruins, *1798*

Meanwhile, some seventy years later, Gustave Doré illustrated London as he imagined it would look in the twenty-first century, resembling a latter-day version of ancient Rome, complete with a New Zealander, an inhabitant of the country that in Doré's day was thought to represent the future, sketching the ruins of the then brand-new Cannon Street station – much as Englishmen had once gone to Athens or Rome to sketch the Parthenon or Colosseum.

From the eighteenth century onwards, animated by similar emotions, travellers set out on journeys to contemplate ruins of the past: Troy, Corinth, Paestum, Thebes, Mycenae, Knossos, Palmyra, Baalbec, Petra and Pompeii. The Germans, masters at formulating compound words for fugitive and rare states of the soul (*Weltschmerz, Schadenfreude, Wanderlust*) coined new terms to describe the feeling for old stones: *Ruinenempfindsamkeit, Ruinensehnsucht, Ruinenlust*. In March 1787, Goethe made two visits to Pompeii. 'Many a calamity has happened in the world,' he reported from Naples, 'but never one that has caused so much entertainment to posterity as this one.' 'What wonderful mornings I have spent in the Colosseum, lost in some corner of those vast ruins!' remembered Stendhal in his *Promenades dans Rome* (1829) and recommended ruin-gazing as 'the most intense pleasure that memory can procure'. He even proposed that the Colosseum was more attractive in ruins than it could ever have been when new.

'My name is Ozymandias, king of kings / Look on my works, ye Mighty, and despair!' reads an inscription on the pedestal of a statue of Ramses II of Egypt in Shelley's 'Ozymandias' (1818). But there is no need for the mighty, or even the humble, to despair. Ramses II lies in pieces on the ground: 'Round the decay / Of that colossal wreck, boundless and bare / The lone and level sands stretch far away.'

Ruins speak of the folly of giving up our peace of mind for the

Gustave Doré, The New Zealander, 1871

Above: *David Roberts*, General View of Baalbec, *1842*
Left: *David Roberts*, Doorway at Baalbec, *1842*

unstable rewards of earthly power. In beholding old stones we may feel our anxieties about our achievements – and lack of them – slacken. What will it matter if we have not succeeded in the eyes of others, if there are no monuments or processions in our honour and if no one smiled at us at a recent gathering? Everything is in any case fated to disappear and New Zealanders will in time be sketching the ruins of our boulevards and offices. Judged against eternity, how little of what agitates us can matter.

Ruins bid us to surrender our strivings and our images of perfection and fulfilment. They remind us that we cannot defy time and that we are the playthings of forces of destruction which can at best be kept at bay but never vanquished. We may enjoy local victories, a few years in which we are able to impose a degree of order upon the chaos, but everything is ultimately fated to slop back into a primeval soup. If this prospect has a power to console, it is perhaps because the greater part of our anxieties stems from an exaggerated sense of the importance of our projects and concerns. We are tortured by our ideals, and by a punishingly high-minded sense of the gravity of what we are doing.

Christian moralists have hence long understood that, to reassure the anxious, it may be best to emphasize that, contrary to what an optimistic mindset teaches us, everything will in fact turn out for the worst: the ceiling will cave in, the bank will lie in ruins, we will die, everyone we love will vanish and all our achievements and even our names will be stamped into the ground. If the idea brings comfort, it may be because something within us instinctively recognizes how closely our miseries are bound up with the grandiosity of our ambitions. To consider our petty status-worries from the perspective of a thousand years hence is to be granted a rare, tranquillizing glimpse of our own insignificance.

7

Vast landscapes can have an anxiety-reducing effect similar to ruins, for they are the representatives of infinite space, as ruins are the representatives of infinite time, against which our weak, short-lived bodies seem no less inconsequential than those of moths or spiders.

Figure 3

Whatever differences exist between people, they are as nothing next to the differences between the most powerful humans and the great deserts, high mountains, glaciers and oceans of the world. There are natural phenomena so large as to make the variations between any two people seem mockingly small. By spending time in vast spaces, a sense of our insignificance in the social hierarchy can be subsumed in a consoling sense of the insignificance of all humans within the cosmos.

We can overcome a feeling of unimportance not by making ourselves more important but by recognizing the relative unimportance of everyone. Our concern with who is a few millimetres taller than us (Figure 3) can give way to an awe for things 1,000 million times larger than us, a force which we may be moved to call infinity, eternity – or simply, and perhaps most usefully, God (Figure 4).

Figure 4

8

A fine remedy for anxieties about insignificance may be to travel – in reality or in works of art – through the gigantic spaces of the world.

Frederic Edwin Church, Niagara, *1857*

Thomas Moran, Nearing Camp, Evening on the Upper Colorado River, Wyoming, *1882*

Albert Bierstadt, Western Landscape, *1869*

Community

1

According to one influential wing of modern secular society, there are few more disreputable fates than to end up being 'like everyone else'; for 'everyone else' is a category that comprises the mediocre and the conformist, the boring and the suburban. The goal of all right-thinking people should be to mark themselves off from the crowd and 'stand out' in whatever way their talents allow.

2

But being like everyone else is not, to follow Christian thought, any sort of calamity, for it was one of Jesus's central claims that all human beings, including the slow-witted, the untalented and the obscure, are creatures of God and loved by him – and are hence deserving of the honour owed to every example of the Lord's work. In the words of St Peter, each of us has the capacity to be a partaker 'of the divine nature' – an idea which audaciously challenges the assumption that certain people are born to mediocrity and others to glory. There are no humans outside the circle of God's love, Christianity insists, attributing divine authority to the notion of mutual respect. What we have in common with others comprises what is most cherishable in ourselves.

Christianity bids us to look beneath the surface differences between people in order to focus on what it considers to be a number of universal truths on which a sense of community and kinship can be built. Some of us may be cruel or impatient, dim or dull, but what should detain and bind us together is the recognition of shared vulnerabilities. Beneath our flaws, there are always two ingredients: fear and a desire for love.

To encourage fellow-feeling, Jesus urged us to learn to look at grown-ups as we might look at children. Few things can more quickly transform our sense of someone's character than to picture them as a child. From this perspective, we are more ready to express the sympathy and generosity we almost naturally display towards the young, whom we call naughty rather than bad, and cheeky rather than arrogant. It can be as hard to hate a child as it can to hate some-one we see sleeping. With their eyes closed and their features relaxed and defenceless, sleepers invite a care and a kind of love – so much so that it is embarrassing to gaze at length at a person asleep beside us on a train or plane. Their face prompts us to an intimacy which throws into question the edifice of civilized indifference on which ordinary communal relations are built. But there is no such thing as a stranger, a Christian would insist, there can only be an impression of strangeness born out of failure to acknowledge that others share in our own needs and weaknesses. Nothing could be more noble, or more fully human, than to perceive that we are indeed fundamentally, where it matters, just like everyone else.

3

The idea that other people might be neither incomprehensible nor distasteful carries weighty implications for our concern with status, given that the desire to achieve social distinction is to a large extent fuelled by a feeling of horror at what might be entailed by being ordinary. The more humiliating, shallow, debased or ugly we take ordinary lives to be, the stronger will be our desire to set ourselves apart. The more corrupt the community, the stronger the lure of individual achievement.

Since its beginnings, Christianity has attempted to enhance, both in practical and in theoretical terms, our sense of the value of belonging to a community; and one way it has done so is through the ritual of the Church service and performances of Church music – occasions when large groups of strangers may feel their suspicions of others abate thanks to a transcendent intermediary.

We might imagine joining an unfamiliar congregation within the walls of a cathedral to hear Bach's *Mass in B Minor* ('the greatest work of music of all ages and of all peoples', Hans-Georg Nägeli, 1817). Much may separate us: age, income, clothes and background. We may never have spoken to one another and be wary of letting others catch our gaze. But as the *Mass* begins, so too does a process of social alchemy. The music gives expression to feelings that had hitherto seemed inchoate and private, and our eyes may fill with tears of relief and gratitude that the composer and musicians have made audible, and hence available to us and others, the movements of our souls. Violins, voices, flutes, double basses, oboes, bassoons and trumpets combine to create sounds that exteriorize the most intimate, elusive areas of our psyches. Furthermore, the public nature of the performance helps us to realize that if others are responding as we are to the music, then they cannot be the in-comprehensible figures we might previously have imagined them to be. Their emotions run along the same tracks as do ours, they are stirred by the very same things and so, whatever the differences in appearance and manner, we share a common core, upon which a connection can be forged and extended far beyond the performance of the *Mass* itself. A group of strangers, so foreign in initial appear-ance, may with time, through the power of choral music, acquire some of the apparent intimacy of friends; we slip behind the stony façades and share, if only briefly, in a beguiling vision of our fellows.

4

But, of course, our sense of what other people are like is seldom as flattering as it can be in a cathedral. The public arena is usually more decrepit and frightening, contributing to an impulse to achieve physical and psychological independence from it.

There are countries where the communal provision of housing, transport, education or health-care is such that citizens will naturally seek to escape involvement with the group and barricade themselves behind solid walls. The desire for high status is never stronger than when being ordinary entails leading a life which fails to cater to a median need for dignity and comfort.

Then there are communities, far rarer, many of them imbued with a strong (often Protestant) Christian heritage, where the public realm exudes respect in its principles and architecture, and where the need to escape into a private domain is therefore less intense. Citizens may lose some of their ambitions for personal glory when the public spaces and facilities of a city are themselves glorious to behold. Simply being an ordinary citizen can seem like an adequate destiny. In Switzerland's largest city, the urge to own a car and avoid sharing a bus or train with strangers loses some of the urgency it may have in Los Angeles or London, thanks to Zurich's superlative tram network – clean, safe, warm and edifying in its punctuality and technical prowess. There is little reason to travel alone when, for only a few francs, an efficient, stately tramway will transport one across the city at a level of comfort an emperor would have envied.

An insight to be drawn from Christianity and applied to communal ethics is that, in so far as we can recover a sense of the preciousness of every human being and, more importantly, in so far as we can legislate for spaces and manners that carry such an awareness in their make-up, then the notion of the ordinary will shed its darker associations, and, correspondingly, the desire to triumph and insulate oneself behind solid walls will weaken – to the psychological benefit of all.

In an ideal Christian community, the dread of what it will be like to live beside the winners will be tempered and contained by a basic equality of dignity and resources. The dichotomy – to succeed and flourish or to fail and wither – will lose some of its excruciating sharpness.

Twin Cities

1

A central theme within Christianity can be traced back to Jesus's career choice. The carpenters of Galilee practised a semi-skilled but insecure and rarely lucrative trade. And yet Jesus was also, in the words of St Peter, 'the right hand of heaven', the son of God, the king of kings, sent to save us from our sins. That someone could combine within himself two such different identities, being at once an itinerant tradesman and the holiest of men, forms the basis upon which the Christian understanding of status is built. Every person possesses, according to this schema, two wholly unrelated kinds of status: earthly status, determined by occupation, income and the opinions of others; and spiritual status, determined by the quality of one's soul and by one's merit in the eyes of God after the Day of Judgement. One might be powerful and revered in the earthly realm, while barren and corrupt in the spiritual one. Or, like the beggar Lazarus in the Gospel of St Luke, one might have only rags to one's name while glorying in divine riches.

In *The City of God* (AD 427), St Augustine explained that all human actions could be interpreted from either a Christian or a Roman perspective, and that the very things esteemed so highly by the Romans – amassing money, building villas, winning wars – counted for nothing in the Christian schema, while a new set of concerns – loving one's neighbours, practising humility and charity, and recognizing one's dependence on God – offered the keys to elevated Christian status. Augustine's embodiment of these two value systems in what he termed two cities, the City of God and the Earthly City, was followed by the claim that the two cities were (until the Day of Judgement) coexistent but separate: one might be a king of the

Earthly City and, at the same time, a manservant in the heavenly one.

It was Dante who further fleshed out Augustine's ideas by offering a detailed account of who would end up where in that ultimate embodiment of the Christian hierarchy: heaven and hell. In the *Divine Comedy* (1315), he enumerated the existence of no fewer than nine different circles of hell (with seventeen separate rings), each one reserved for a particular kind of sin, and at the same time of ten different spheres of heaven, each one reserved for a particular kind of virtue. The religious hierarchy resembled a distorted or inverted version of its secular counterpart. Hell was home to a range of individuals who had once had high status: generals, writers, poets, emperors, bishops, popes and businessmen – now stripped of their privileges and enduring extreme sufferings for having offended God's laws. In the fourth ring of the ninth circle of hell, Dante came upon the screams of those who had been powerful but treacherous in life and were now being chewed in the mouth of the three-headed giant Lucifer. In the first ring of the seventh circle, the poet found himself by a river of boiling blood, in which Alexander the Great and Attila the Hun struggled to stay afloat, while on the river bank a group of centaurs fired arrows over their heads to force them back into the sickening froth. In the fifth circle, a range of angry, prominent authority figures whose tempers had cost the lives of others languished in a swampy, fetid cesspool and choked on mud, while in the third circle excrement rained down upon those who had been gluttonous when alive.

The discrepancy between people's heavenly and earthly status offered believers a way out of an oppressive, one-dimensional vision of success. Christianity did not do away with the concept of a hierarchy, its contribution was rather to redefine success and failure in an ethical, non-material way – to insist that poverty could coexist with goodness, a humble occupation with a noble soul: 'A man's life consisteth not in the abundance of the things which he possesseth,'

Gustave Doré, The Violent Tortured in the Rain of Fire, *1861*

Gustave Doré, The Thieves Tortured by Serpents, *1861*

knew St Luke, the follower of the impecunious carpenter from Galilee.

2

But far from merely asserting the superiority of spiritual over material success, Christianity also endowed the values it revered with a seductive seriousness and beauty – and it did so in part through the magisterial use of painting, literature, music and architecture. It employed works of art to make a case for virtues which had never before loomed large in the sense of priorities of rulers or their people.

For centuries, the talents of the finest stonemasons, poets, musicians and painters – who had once been called upon to celebrate the glories of emperors and blood-curdling victories of legions over barbarian hordes – were directed towards praising such activities as offering charity and respecting the poor. The glorification of worldly values did not of course disappear in the Christian era – there remained plenty of palaces to remind the world of the charms of mercantile or landed wealth and power – but, for a time at least, in many communities, the most impressive buildings on the horizon were those that celebrated the nobility of poverty rather than the might of a royal family or corporation, and the most moving pieces of music sang not of personal fulfilment but of the torment of the son of God, who had been:

> despised and rejected of men;
> a man of sorrows, and acquainted with grief.
> Isaiah 53.3–5; G.F. Handel, *Messiah* (1741)

Through its command of aesthetic resources, of buildings, paintings and Masses, Christianity created a bulwark against the

authority of earthly values and kept its spiritual concerns at the forefront of the mind and the eye.

In the four centuries between approximately 1130 and 1530, in
towns and cities across Europe, over a hundred cathedrals were
erected, their spires dominating the skyscape, looming above grain-
stores, palaces, offices, factories and homes. They had a grandeur
that few other buildings could rival; they provided an environment
where people from every walk of life could gather and think about
what were, in the context of the history of architecture, some highly
unusual ideas: about the value of sadness and innocence, meekness
and pity. Whereas a city's other buildings serviced earthly needs –
housing and feeding the body, allowing it to rest, contributing
machines and implements to assist it – the unique function of
cathedrals was to empty the mind of egoistic projects and lead it
towards God and his love. City dwellers engaged in worldly tasks
could, during the course of a day, on seeing the outline of these giant
structures, remind themselves of a vision of life which challenged
the authority of ordinary ambitions. A cathedral like that of
Chartres, whose spires soar 105 metres into the sky, the height of a
thirty-four-floor skyscraper, was understood to be the home of the
dispossessed, a symbol of the wonders they would enjoy in the next
life. However ramshackle their physical dwellings might be, the
cathedral was where they belonged at heart. Its beauties reflected
their inner worth; its stained-glass windows and ceilings made vivid
the glory of Jesus's message to them.

3

Christianity did not, of course, ever succeed in abolishing the
Earthly City and its values, and yet if we retain a distinction between
wealth and virtue, and still ask of people whether they are good
rather than simply important, it is in large part due to the impres-

sion left upon Western consciousness by a religion which, for centuries, lent its resources and prestige to the defence of a handful of extraordinary ideas about the rightful distribution of status. It was the genius of the artists and craftsmen who worked in the service of Christianity to give an enduring form to their religion's values and to make these real to us through their handling of stone, glass, sound, word and image.

In a world where secular buildings relentlessly whisper to us of the importance of earthly power, the cathedrals on the skylines of great towns and cities may continue to provide an imaginative holding space for the priorities of the spirit.

V.
BOHEMIA

Lee Miller, Le Déjeuner sur L'Herbe, *1937. A group of Surrealist friends at a picnic in Mougins, France. On the left, Nusch and Paul Eluard. On the right, from bottom, Ady Fidelin, Man Ray and Roland Penrose.*

1

At the start of the nineteenth century, a new group of people began to be noticed in Western Europe and the United States. They often dressed simply, they lived in the cheaper parts of town, they read a lot, they seemed not to care too much about money, many were of melancholic temperament, their allegiances were to art and emotion rather than to business and material success, they sometimes had unconventional sexual lives, some of the women had short hair before it was the fashion – and they came to be described as 'bohemian'. The word had traditionally been used to refer to gypsies, who were mistakenly thought to have originated in central Europe but – especially following the success of *Scènes de la vie de Bohême* (1851), Henri Murger's account of life in the garrets and cafés of Paris – the word came to be used in relation to a range of people who did not, for one reason or another, fit the bourgeois conception of respectability.

From the outset, bohemia was a broad church. Early writers argued that bohemians were to be found in every social class, age group and profession: men and women, rich and poor, poets and lawyers, scientists and the unemployed. Arthur Ransome, in *Bohemia in London* (1907), remarked, 'Bohemia can be anywhere: it is not a place but an attitude of mind.' There have been bohemians in Cambridge, Massachusetts, and in Venice Beach, California; there have been bohemians with servants and others in huts on the shores of quiet lakes; there have been guitar players and biologists; there have been outwardly conventional ones and others with a taste for bathing naked by moonlight. One can wind the word around a number of different artistic and social phenomena of the last two hundred years, from Romanticism to Surrealism, from the Beatniks to the Punks, from the Situationists to the Kibbutzniks, and still not snap a thread binding something important together.

In London in 1929, the bohemian poet Brian Howard invited his friends to a party and on the invitation card printed a list of his likes and dislikes – which, in spite of their particularly English early twentieth-century features, afford us a flavour of some of the characteristic inclinations and fears that bohemians have manifested throughout their history:

J'ACCUSE	J'ADORE
Ladies and Gentlemen	Men and Women
Public Schools	Nietzsche
Debutantes	Picasso
Sadist devotees of blood-sports	Kokoschka
'Eligible bachelors'	Jazz
Missionaries	Acrobats
People who worry they can't meet so-and-so because they've got 'a bad reputation'	The Mediterranean
	D. H. Lawrence
	Havelock Ellis
The young men one meets at boring parties in stuck-up moronic country houses	The sort of people who know they haven't got immortal souls; and are not anticipating – after death – any rubbishy reunion, apotheosis or ANYTHING

What Brian Howard and his fellow bohemians disliked might more succinctly have been summed up with a single term: the bourgeoisie. Having come to prominence in the same historical period, in France, after the fall of Napoleon in 1815, bohemians claimed a ferocious dislike of almost everything the bourgeois stood for, and prided themselves on the extravagance of their insults against them.

'Hatred of the bourgeois is the beginning of wisdom,' wrote Gustave Flaubert, a standard utterance for a mid-nineteenth-century French writer, for whom such disdain was as much a badge of one's profession as having an affair with an actress and making a trip to the orient. Flaubert accused the bourgeois of extreme prudery and materialism, of being at once cynical and sentimental, of immersing themselves in trivia, of spending an age, for example, debating whether melon was a vegetable or a fruit and whether it should be eaten as a starter (the French way) or as a dessert (the English way). Stendhal, no fonder of this class, asserted, 'The conversation of the true bourgeois about men and life, which is no more than a collection of ugly details, brings on a profound attack of spleen when I am obliged to listen to it for any length of time.'

But what ultimately separated bohemia from the bourgeoisie was not the choice of conversational topics or desserts, but the answer to the question of who deserved high status and for what reason. From the outset, bohemians were those who, whether they owned a mansion or a garret, pitted themselves against the economic, meritocratic status system to which the early nineteenth century gave birth.

2

At the heart of the conflict lay a contrasting assessment of the value of worldly achievement on the one hand and sensitivity on the other. Whereas the bourgeoisie accorded status on the basis of commercial success and public reputation, for bohemians what mattered above all else, and certainly above the ability to pay for an elegant home or clothes, was to be receptive to the world and to devote oneself, as a spectator or creator, to the primary repository of feeling: art. The martyr figures of the bohemian value system were those who had sacrificed the security of a regular job and the esteem of their society in order to write, paint or make music, or devote themselves to travel or to their friends and families. They might, because of their commitments, be lacking signs of outward decency and yet they were still, bohemians averred, worthy of the highest honour, because of their ethical good sense and their powers of receptivity and expression.

Many bohemians were prepared to suffer or even starve for their impractical beliefs. In the paintings that depicted them in the nineteenth century, they were often to be found slouched on a chair in the dirty attic rooms of apartment blocks. They appeared gaunt and exhausted. There might be a faraway look in their eyes and a skull on their bookshelves. They might be wearing an expression to frighten a factory foreman or office manager – signs that their souls were not taken up with the shallow utilitarian concerns they accused the bourgeoisie of harbouring.

What had led to such destitution was a horror of devoting one's life to a job one despised. Charles Baudelaire declared that all jobs were soul-destroying, aside from that of being a poet and – even less plausibly – a 'warrior'. When Marcel Duchamp visited New York in 1915, he described Greenwich Village as 'a true Bohemia' because the place was, he said, 'full of people doing *nothing*'. Half a century later Jack Kerouac, addressing an audience in a West Coast piano bar, spoke out against 'the commuters with their tight collars obliged to catch the 5.48 a.m. train at Millbrae or San Carlos to get to work in San Francisco', praising instead the free spirits, bums, poets, beats and artists who slept late and burned their work clothes in order to become 'sons of the road and watch the freight trains pass, take in

Formerly attributed to Géricault, now unknown,
Portrait of an Artist in his Studio, *c. 1820*

Gustave Courbet, Portrait of the Artist (Man with a Pipe), *c. 1848–9*

the immensity of the sky and feel the weight of ancestral America'.

Though bohemians did not argue that there was a theoretical incompatibility between having an intense life of the mind and owning a successful law firm or factory, most implied that there might be one in practice. In the preface to *On Love* (1822), Stendhal explained that he had attempted to write clearly and for a broad audience, but that he could not give 'hearing to the deaf nor sight to the blind'. 'So people with money and coarse pursuits, who have made 100,000 francs in the year before they open this book, had better close it again quickly, particularly if they are bankers, manufacturers or respectable industrialists ... The active, hardworking, eminently respectable and positive life of a privy councillor, a textile manufacturer or a clever banker reaps its reward in wealth but not in tender sensations. Little by little the hearts of these gentlemen ossify. People who pay 2,000 workmen at the end of every week do not *waste their time* like this; their minds are always bent on useful and positive things.' Stendhal felt his book would be best appreciated by those who had a taste for indolence, liked daydreaming, welcomed the emotions sparked by listening to Mozart's operas and could be thrown into hours of bittersweet thoughts after just one glimpse of a beautiful face in a crowded street.

The idea that money and practical occupations corrupt the soul or, in Stendhal's words the capacity for 'tender sensations', has reverberated down the history of bohemia. It can, for example, be heard no less clearly over a hundred and forty years after Stendhal's lament in Charles Bukowski's poem 'Something for the Touts, the Nuns, the Grocery Clerks and You' (1965), which evoked the lives of wealthy businessmen:

> with bad breath and big feet, men
> who look like frogs, hyenas, men who walk
> as if melody had never been invented, men

who think it is intelligent to hire and fire and
profit, men with expensive wives they possess
like sixty acres of ground to be drilled
or shown-off or to be walled away from
the incompetent ...
... men who stand in front of
windows thirty feet wide and see nothing,
men with luxury yachts who can sail around
the world and yet never get out of their vest
pockets, men like snails, men like eels, men
like slugs, and not as good.

Just as money cannot confer honour in the bohemian value
system, neither can possessions. Through bohemian eyes, yachts and
mansions are symbols of arrogance and frivolity. Bohemian status is
more likely to be earned through an inspired conversational style or
the authorship of an intelligent, heartfelt volume of poetry.

In July 1845, one of the most renowned bohemians of nineteenth-
century America, Henry Thoreau, moved into a log cabin he had
built with his own hands on the north shore of Walden Pond, near
the town of Concord, Massachusetts. His goal was to see if he could
lead an outwardly plain but inwardly rich existence, and in the
process demonstrate to the bourgeoisie that it was possible to combine a life of material scarcity with psychological fulfilment. Proving
just how cheaply one could subsist once one had ceased to worry
about impressing others, Thoreau gave his readers a breakdown of
the minimal costs he had incurred in building his cabin:

Boards,	$8 03	Mostly shanty boards
Refuse shingles for roof and sides,	4 00	
Laths,	1 25	
Two second-hand windows with glass,	2 43	
One thousand old bricks,	4 00	
Two casks of lime,	2 40	That was high
Hair,	0 31	More than I needed
Mantle-tree iron,	0 15	
Nails,	3 90	
Hinges and screws,	0 14	
Latch,	0 10	
Chalk,	0 01	I carried a good part
Transportation,	1 40	on my back
In all,	$ 28.12	

'Most of the luxuries, and many of the so-called comforts of life, are not only not indispensable, but positive hindrances to the elevation of mankind,' wrote Thoreau, adding, in an attempt to upset his society's connection between owning things and being honourable, 'Man is rich in proportion to the number of things he can do without.'

Thoreau tried to reconfigure our sense of what having little money could indicate about a person. It was not, as the bourgeois perspective tended subtly to suggest, always a sign of being a loser at the game of life. Having little money might simply mean that one had opted to focus one's energies on activities other than business, growing rich in things other than cash in the process. Instead of using the word poverty to describe his condition, Thoreau preferred the word simplicity – this, he felt, conveyed a consciously chosen rather than an imposed material situation, a simplicity which, he reminded the merchants of Boston, people no less noble than 'the Chinese, Hindoo, Persian and Greek philosophers' had once willingly practised. After

WALDEN;

OR,

LIFE IN THE WOODS.

By HENRY D. THOREAU,

AUTHOR OF "A WEEK ON THE CONCORD AND MERRIMACK RIVERS."

I do not propose to write an ode to dejection, but to brag as lustily as chanticleer in the morning, standing on his roost, if only to wake my neighbors up. — Page 92.

BOSTON:

TICKNOR AND FIELDS.

M DCCC LIV.

Title page of the first edition of Henry Thoreau's Walden, *1854* his stay on the shores of Walden Pond, the tenor of the message that Thoreau delivered to the burgeoning industrialized society of the United States would have been familiar to almost all bohemians before and after him. As he put it, 'Money is not required to buy one necessary of the soul.'

3

An insight of bohemians has been that our ability to maintain confidence in a way of life at odds with the mainstream culture greatly depends on the value system operating in our immediate environment, on the kind of people we mix with socially and on what we read and listen to.

They have recognized that our peace of mind can be only too easily shattered and our commitments challenged by a few minutes of conversation with an acquaintance who feels, even if he or she does not say, that money and a public profile are ultimately estimable – or by reading a magazine which, by reporting only on the feats of bourgeois heroes, insidiously undermines the worth of any alternative ambitions.

Bohemians have in consequence tended to display particular care when choosing who to spend their time with. Some, like Thoreau, have escaped the corrupting influences of society altogether. Others have been assiduous in creating communities of congenial spirits, refusing to accept the kind of social life that tends naturally to befall us when we socialize with many of the characters whom we are thrown together with at school, and in families and workplaces.

In the world's large cities, bohemians have clustered in certain districts to ensure that their daily contacts will be with genuine rather than status-concerned friends. The history of bohemia is studded with names of places rendered famous by the friendships they hosted: Montparnasse, Bloomsbury, Chelsea, Greenwich Village, Venice Beach.

The photographer Lee Miller and her friend the model Tanja Ramm in Miller's studio in Montparnasse, Paris, 1931

4

Bohemians have also carefully redefined their understanding of the word failure. According to the bourgeois ideology, a financial or critical failure in business or the arts must function as a significant indictment of one's character, given the ideology's accompanying assumption that society is essentially fair in distributing its rewards.

But bohemians have refused such a punitive interpretation of outward failure by focusing on how often the world is governed by idiocy and prejudice. Given human nature, they have reasoned that those who succeed in society will rarely be the wisest or the best, they will be those who can pander most effectively to the flawed values of their audiences. There may indeed – bohemians have suggested – be no more damning sign of a person's ethical and imaginative limitation than a capacity for commercial success.

Such a perspective explains the interest and respect accorded by many nineteenth-century bohemians to figures from politics and the arts whose lives could only have been described as failures according to a bourgeois scale of values. The most celebrated of these figures was the minor English poet Thomas Chatterton, who committed suicide in 1770 at the age of eighteen, worn down by poverty and the rejection of his work by his patrons. Alfred de Vigny's play *Chatterton*, first performed in Paris in 1835, turned the young poet into a mouthpiece for all the values that bohemia held dear. The play celebrated personal inspiration over tradition, kindness over financial advantage, intensity and madness over rationality and utilitarianism. De Vigny's message was that gifted, sensitive poets were almost fated to be driven to despair and even suicide by the crassness of their bourgeois public.

The myth of the misunderstood outsider who is nevertheless, despite rejection, superior to the insider, reflected or shaped the lives of many of the greatest figures of bohemia. Gérard de Nerval, a poet more talented than Chatterton but no happier, hanged himself,

Henry Wallis, The Death of Chatterton, *1855–6*

destitute and mad, at the age of forty-seven in 1855. Summing up the experiences of his generation of sensitive brethren whose talents and temperaments had made them unfit for the bourgeois world, de Nerval wrote: 'Ambition was not of our age ... and the greedy race for position and honours drove us away from spheres of political activity. There remained to us only the poet's ivory tower where we mounted ever higher to isolate ourselves from the crowd. In those high altitudes we breathed at last the pure air of solitude; we drank forgetfulness in the golden cup of legend; we were drunk with poetry and love.'

When Edgar Allan Poe died in 1849 at the age of thirty-seven, he too was absorbed into the bohemian story of noble failure. In an essay on his life and works, Charles Baudelaire wrote that Poe's fate was typical of that of gifted men forced to dwell among brutes. Baudelaire cursed the tenor of public opinion in democratic societies like the United States, warning that one could expect no charity or indulgence from it. Indeed, he wrote, poets 'cannot hope to fit in, either in a democratic or an aristocratic society, in a republic or an absolute monarchy ... illustrious unfortunates, [they are] born to suffer the harsh apprenticeship of genius amidst the crowd of mediocre souls'.

The moral Baudelaire drew from Poe's life was to be a recurring one in the French poet's work, finding its most crystalline expression in the sad flappings of his famous seabird:

The Albatross

Often, to pass the time, sailors
Will catch albatrosses, those great seabirds
Which nonchalantly chaperone ships
Across bitter gulfs.

Hardly have they set them down on the deck
Than these monarchs of the sky, awkward and ashamed,
Piteously let their great white wings
Drag at their sides like pairs of unshipped oars.

How gauche and weak becomes this winged traveller!
How weak and awkward, even comical
He who was but lately so adroit!
One deckhand teases his beak with a branding iron,
Another mimics, by limping, the cripple that once flew!

The Poet is like this sovereign of the clouds,
Riding the storm above the marksman's range;
In exile on earth, hooted and jeered at,
He cannot walk because of his great wings.

By emphasizing the dignity and superiority of the rejected one, bohemia offered a secular counterpart to the Christian account of Jesus's ostracism and crucifixion. Like the Christian pilgrim, the bohemian poet would be tortured by the uncomprehending masses but, as in the Christian story, neglect was in itself evidence of the superiority of the neglected party. That one is not understood is a sign that there is much to understand. It is because of his great wings that the poet cannot walk.

5

Alongside the bohemian belief in the inferiority of the group and its traditions came a stress on the superiority of the individual and so an enthusiasm for splitting off from convention. 'No more rules,' cried Victor Hugo in the preface to *Hernani* (1830). 'For talent to surrender personal originality would be like God becoming a servant.'

A similar rallying cry reverberated through Ralph Waldo Emerson's essay *Self-Reliance* (1840): 'Whoso would be a man must be a non-conformist.' By fitting in with others' ideas of how to live, dress, eat or write, one would, said Emerson, slowly acquire an 'asinine expression'. Every noble person was to be guided by the dictum: 'What I must do is all that concerns me, not what the people think.' 'I hope in these days we have heard the last of conformity and consistency,' concluded Emerson. 'Let the words be gazetted and ridiculous henceforward … Let us never bow and apologize more … Let us affront and reprimand the smooth mediocrity and squalid contentment of the times.'

Hugo's and Emerson's calls to break free from tradition fell upon receptive ears. In 1850, Gérard de Nerval ceased conforming to existing ideas of suitable pets and acquired a lobster, which he led around the Jardin du Luxembourg on the end of a blue ribbon. 'Why should a lobster be any more ridiculous than a dog,' he questioned, 'or any other animal that one chooses to take for a walk? I have a liking for lobsters. They are peaceful, serious creatures. They know the secrets of the sea, they don't bark, and they don't gnaw upon one's monadic privacy like dogs do. And Goethe had an aversion to dogs, and he wasn't mad.'

Being a great and original artist became synonymous with surprising or, even better, offending the bourgeoisie. On completing his novel *Salammbô* (1862), Flaubert declared that he had written his book in order to '(1) annoy the bourgeois, (2) unnerve and shock sensitive people (3) irritate the archaeologists, (4) seem unintelligible to the ladies, and (5) earn me a reputation as a pederast and a cannibal'.

In the 1850s, a group of bohemian students in Paris began a club which they hoped would 'offend judges and pharmacists'. Having discerned a most effective way of achieving their ends, they named themselves the Suicide Club and issued a manifesto declaring that all members would be dead by their own hands before the age of thirty – or before they went bald, whichever came first. Only one suicide was reported among the members, but the club was deemed a success nevertheless after an outraged politician in the Chamber of Deputies made a speech declaring it to be an 'immoral and illegal monstrosity'.

The history of bohemia is studded with attempts to irritate the respectable classes. In New York in 1917, a group of artists decided to secede from bourgeois life and called for the creation of a 'free and independent republic of Greenwich Village', which would be dedicated to art, love, beauty and cigarettes. To mark the birth of their breakaway state, the group climbed to the top of the Washington Square Arch, drank whiskey, fired cap pistols and read out a declaration of independence, which consisted simply of the word 'whereas' uttered in rapid succession. Recalling the event many years later, one member of the new republic (which lasted until dawn) remarked, 'We were radicals devoted to anything – so long as it was taboo in the Mid-West.'

Unfortunately for bohemians, the more they have shocked the bourgeoisie the weaker has been the willingness or capacity of the bourgeoisie to be shocked – which has forced them to perform increasingly extreme antics, as the history of twentieth-century bohemian movements testifies.

'Intelligent man is now a standard type,' declared Dada's founder, Tristan Tzara, in Zurich in 1915, 'but the thing we are short of is the *idiotic*. Dada is using all its strength to establish the idiotic everywhere.' To this end, Dadaists took to entering smart Zurich restaurants in order to shout 'Dada' at bourgeois diners. The Dada artist Marcel Duchamp painted a moustache on a *Mona Lisa* and named his work *L.H.O.O.Q.* (*Elle a chaud au cul* / She has a hot arse.)

The Dada poet Hugo Ball pioneered a meaningless, multilingual

poetry and delivered the first example, 'Karawane', in a Zurich nightclub dressed in a suit made out of shiny blue cardboard, with a witch's hat on his head.

KARAWANE
jolifanto bambla ô falli bambla
grossiga m'pfa habla horem
égiga goramen
higo bloiko russula huju
hollaka hollala
anlogo bung
blago bung
blago bung
bosso fataka
ü üü ü
schampa wulla wussa ólobo
hej tatta gôrem
eschige zunbada
wulubu ssubudu uluw ssubudu
tumba ba- umf
kusagauma
ba - umf

Looking back at the ambitions of Dada, the one-time Dadaist painter Hans Richter remarked: 'We wanted to bring forward a new kind of human being, free from the tyranny of rationality, of banality, of generals, fatherlands, nations, art-dealers, microbes, residence permits and the past. To outrage public opinion was our basic principle.'

Other groups followed in Dada's footsteps. In 1924, the Surrealists opened the Bureau of Surrealist Enquiries in the rue de Grenelle in Paris. A dress-shop dummy hung from the ceiling in the window, and members of the public were invited to bring in stories of dreams and coincidences and new ideas they might have about politics, art and fashion. These were then typed up and stuck around the walls. Antonin Artaud, the director of the Bureau, proclaimed, 'We need *disturbed* followers far more than we need active followers.'

In 1932, no less keen to offend the bourgeoisie, the Italian Futurist Filippo Marinetti published *The Futurist Cookbook*, designed, he wrote, to revolutionize the way that Italians ate and to pull them away from nineteenth-century culinary tastes, in particular, that for pasta (he cited *maccheroni al ragù* and *tagliatelle alla bolognese* as epitomes of bourgeois anachronism). But to anyone who bought the cookbook hoping for inspiration, it became evident that Marinetti was – no less than Gérard de Nerval or Antonin Artaud – out to upset expectations. Recipes included:

Strawberry Breasts: 'A pink plate with two erect feminine breasts made of ricotta dyed pink with Campari and nipples of candied strawberry. Further fresh strawberries under the covering of ricotta make it possible to bite into an ideal multiplication of imaginary breasts.'

Aerofood: 'Composed of a slice of fennel, an olive and a kumquat, together with a strip of cardboard, on which should be glued, one next to the other, a piece of velvet, a piece of silk, and a piece of sandpaper. The sandpaper is not be eaten. It is there to be fingered with the right hand while one sucks on the kumquat.'

Cubist Vegetable Patch: '1. Little cubes of celery from Verona fried and sprinkled with paprika. 2. Little cubes of fried carrot sprinkled with grated horse-radish. 3. Boiled peas. 4. Little pickled onions from Ivrea sprinkled with chopped parsley. 5. Little bars of Fontina cheese. N.B. The cubes must not be larger than one cubic centimetre.'

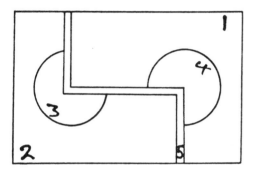

6

The excesses of bohemia are hardly difficult to discern. It is only a short step from valuing originality and emphasizing the non-material aspects of life to feeling that almost anything that could surprise a judge or pharmacist – from crustacean-walking to strawberry-breast-eating – must be important.

So keen have many bohemians been to place spiritual concerns at the forefront of their lives, that their neglect of practical matters has led them into an all-consuming struggle to find enough on which to survive, with less time to think about the spirit and more need to think about the body than even a busy and highly materialistic judge or pharmacist.

In Massachusetts in 1844, a group of utopian bohemian artists set up a communal farm they named Fruitlands, stating that they had no interest in money or work as an end in itself. They only wanted to grow enough to feed the body and then turn their energies to poetry, painting, nature and romantic love. The founder of the community, Bronson Alcott, announced that the mission of the new farmers was 'to *be*, not to *do*'. He and his fellow members subscribed to a range of ambitious ideals typical of bohemian communities before and after: they wore no cotton clothes (slaves picked cotton), didn't eat animals or dairy products and adopted a principally vegan diet – only eating things that grew high up in the air, shunning carrots and potatoes because they pointed down into the ground, rather than aspiring to heaven like apples and pears.

Predictably, the community did not last long. The farmers' reluctance to engage with practicalities led them, once the first summer was over, into an urgent battle to keep body and soul together, rather than to reading Homer and Petrarch, as they had planned. Emerson, who had met Alcott in Boston a few years before the founding of the farm, remarked of Fruitlands' members, 'Their whole doctrine was spiritual, but they always ended up saying, "Could you please send us some more money?"' Six months after Fruitlands began, the community dispersed in acrimony and despair – a familiar bohemian tale of idealism gone sour through an unbending refusal to subscribe to even minimal bourgeois discipline.

It would be senseless and very rare to feel anxiety in relation to the bourgeoisie's conception of status if this class was as misguided and as unimpressive as bohemians are occasionally in danger of making out. While many good ideas have been shocking to Mid-Westerners, it hardly follows that everything that shocks them will be outstanding. It is only because judges and pharmacists do things extremely well that it can be so troubling to feel one might nevertheless have to question or dissent from some aspects of their behaviour and mentality.

7

Which is not to say that one should hold oneself back. Whatever the excesses of the outer wings of bohemia, the movement's enduring contribution has been to provide a range of suggestive challenges to the bourgeoisie's ideals. It has accused them of failing to understand the role that wealth should play in a good life; of being too hasty in condemning worldly failure and too slavish in venerating outward success; of having excessive faith in sham notions of propriety; of dogmatically identifying professional qualifications with talent; of neglecting the value of art, sensitivity, playfulness and creativity; and of being overconcerned with order, rules, bureaucracy and time-keeping.

To sum up its contribution in the broadest, most comprehensive terms, one might simply suggest that bohemia has provided legitimacy for the pursuit of an alternative way of life; it has staked out and defined a subculture where certain of the values underrated or overlooked by the bourgeois mainstream have been granted due authority and prestige.

Like Christianity, for which it has in many ways functioned as an emotional substitute – emerging in the nineteenth century at around the very time when Christianity began to lose its grip on the imagination – bohemia has articulated a case for a spiritual, as opposed to a material, method of evaluating oneself and others. Like Christianity's monasteries and nunneries, bohemia's garrets and cafés, low-rent districts and cooperative businesses have provided a refuge in which that part of the population uninterested in pursuing the bourgeoisie's rewards has found sustenance and fellowship.

Furthermore, the standing of certain bohemian figures has helped to reassure those made most anxious by the dominant status system that to sidestep the mainstream has a long and occasionally distinguished history, stretching back to the poets of nineteenth-century Paris, the playful subversiveness of the Dada movement and the Provençal picnics of the Surrealists.

A way of life which might have seemed wayward and absurd has, thanks to the most talented bohemians, come to seem serious and laudable. To the role-model of the lawyer, the entrepreneur and the scientist, bohemia has added the poet, the traveller and the essayist. It has proposed that these characters too, whatever their eccentricities and material shortfalls, may be worthy of an elevated status of their own.

8

The beginning of a mature solution to status anxiety might be said to begin with the recognition that status is available from a variety of different audiences: from industrialists and from bohemians, from families and from philosophers – and that our choice of audience can be free and willed.

However unpleasant anxieties about status may be, it is difficult to imagine a good life entirely free of them, for a fear that one might fail and disgrace oneself in the eyes of others is only a natural consequence of having ambitions, a preference for one set of outcomes over another and a respect for individuals besides oneself. Status anxiety is the price we pay for acknowledging a public difference between a successful and an unsuccessful life.

Yet, though our need for status may be fixed, we retain a choice of where to fulfil the need, we are free to ensure that our worries about being disgraced will arise principally in relation to a public whose methods of judgement we both understand and respect. Status anxiety could be defined as problematic only in so far as it is inspired by values that we follow because we are fearful and preternaturally obedient, because we have been anaesthetized into believing that they are natural, perhaps God-given, because those around us are in thrall to them or because we have grown too imaginatively timid to conceive of alternatives.

Philosophy, art, politics, Christianity and bohemia did not seek to do away with a status hierarchy; they attempted to institute new kinds of hierarchy based on sets of values unrecognized by, and critical of, those of the majority. While retaining a firm grip on a distinction between success and failure, good and bad, shameful and honourable, these five groups endeavoured to remould our sense of what could rightfully be said to belong under these weighty headings.

In so doing, they helped to lend legitimacy to those who, in every generation, will be unable or unwilling to follow dutifully behind the dominant notions of high status but who may yet deserve to be categorized other than under the brutal epithets of loser or nobody. They have provided us with a set of persuasive and consoling reminders that there is more than one way – and more than a judge or pharmacist's way – of succeeding at life.

ACKNOWLEDGEMENTS

Special thanks to: Simon Prosser, Caroline Dawnay, Nicole Aragi, Dan Frank, Michael Ledger Lomas, Michael Port, Dominic Houlder, Tom Graves, Felicity Harvey and Austin Taylor.

PICTURE ACKNOWLEDGEMENTS

p.27 Punch Ltd.; p.32 AP Photo; p.36 Mary Evans Picture Library; p.38 Stapleton Collection, UK/Bridgeman Art Library; p.39 The Hoover Company; p.41 Reprinted by arrangement with Sears, Roebuck and Co. Protected under copyright. No duplication permitted; pp.42/43 GURSKY © Andreas Gursky/DACS London 2003, Courky Gallery, Monika Sprueth, Cologne; p.49 Galleria dell'Accademia, Venice/Bridgeman Art Library; p.68 The British Library, London; p.69 Corpus Christi College, Oxford/Bridgeman Art Library; p.70 Musée Condé, Chantilly/Bridgeman Art Library; p.90 Bettmann/Corbis; p.146 Jean Siméon Chardin, *The Attentive Muse*, Samuel H. Kress Collection, Image © 2003 Board of Trustees, National Gallery of Art, Washington DC; pp.148/9 Ashmolean Museum, Oxford/Bridgeman Art Library; p.150 National Museum and Gallery of Wales, Cardiff/Bridgeman Art Library; p.151 Museum Oskar Reinhart am Stadtgarten, Winterthur; p.152 Kunstindustrimuseet, Copenhagen/photo: Pernille Klemp; pp.154/5 Nivaagaards Malerisamling, Denmark; p.167 Musée Condé, Chantilly/Bridgeman Art Library; p.168 Musée de la Ville de Paris, Musée Carnavalet, Paris/Bridgeman Art Library; p.170 Louvre, Paris/ Bridgeman Art Library; pp.172/3 Courtesy of the Warden and Scholars of New College, Oxford/Bridgeman Art Library; p.176 Courtesy of the Warden and Scholars of New College, Oxford/Bridgeman Art Library; p.177 Punch Ltd.; p.178t The New Yorker Collection 1995, Peter Steiner from cartoonbank.com. All Rights Reserved; p.178b The New Yorker Collection 1987, J.B. Handelsman from cartoonbank.com. All Rights Reserved; p.179t The New Yorker Collection 1980, Charles Barsotti from cartoonbank.com. All Rights Reserved; p.179m The New Yorker Collection 1988, Bernard Schoenbaum from cartoonbank.com. All Rights Reserved; p.179b The New Yorker Collection 1988, Mike Twohy from cartoonbank.com. All Rights Reserved; p.180 The New Yorker Collection 1998, Michael Crawford from cartoonbank.com. All Rights Reserved; p.181 The New Yorker Collection 1997, Frank Cotham from cartoonbank.com. All Rights Reserved; p.183 The New Yorker Collection 1988, William Hamilton from cartoonbank.com. All Rights Reserved; p.206 Mercedes-Benz/Campbell Dyle Dye; p.219 Intercontinental Hotels Corporation; p.220 Agency Merkley/Newman Harty; p.221 photo: Alan Mahon/Horton Stephens photographer's agents; p.236 Musée de Tesse, Le Mans/Bridgeman Art Library; p.237 Private Collection/ Lauros/ Giraudon/ Bridgeman Art Library; p.241 Louvre, Paris/Bridgeman Art Library; pp.242/3 Courtesy of the Trustees of Sir John Soane's Museum, London/Bridgeman Art Library; p.246 Stapleton Collection, UK/Bridgeman Art Library; p.247 Stapleton Collection, UK/Bridgeman Art Library; pp.250/1 Corcoran Gallery of Art, Washington DC; p.252/3 Bolton Museum & Art Gallery; p.254/5 The Collection of the Newark Museum, Newark NJ. Purchase 1961, The Members' Fund, 61.516; p.269 Lauros/Giraudon/Bridgeman Art Library; p.270 London Aerial Photo Library/Corbis; pp.272/3 Architectural Association Photo Library Mary Parsons; p.276 Lee Miller Archives, Chiddingly, England; p.281 Louvre, Paris/ Bridgeman Art Library; p.282 Musée Fabre, Montpellier/Bridgeman Art Library; p.288 Lee Miller Archives, Chiddingly, England; p.290/1 Yale Center for British Art, Paul Mellon Collection, USA/Bridgeman Art Library; p.296 Galleria Pictogramma, Rome/Bridgeman Art Library / Alinari

INDEX

Page numbers in *italic* indicate illustrations and captions

Abbott, Lyman: *How to Succeed*, 58
achievement: and expectation, 56;
    and status, 5, 193
Acton, Sir William, 213
advertising, 61, 204–8
Aelfric, Abbot of Eynsham:
    Colloquy, 69, 75
agriculture: advances in, 34–5
Alcott, Bronson, 300
Alexander the Great, 119–20, 264
ambition, *219–21*
American National Exhibition,
    Moscow, 1959, *32*, 33
American Revolution (1776), 51
Antisthenes, 120
approval *see* public opinion
aristocracy, 80–81, 83–4
Aristotle: *Eudemian Ethics*, 123;
    Poetics, 159, 163; *Politics*, 48
Armstrong, Archibald, 172
Arnold, Matthew, 133–4, 181;
    Culture and Anarchy, 134–5, 211
art: bohemian idealization of, 280;
    Christian, 267–8; purpose, 133–45
Artaud, Antonin, 298
Astor, John Jacob, 60
Attila the Hun, 264
Augustine, St: *The City of God*, 57,
    263
Austen, Jane, 153; *Mansfield Park*,
    137–40
Automatic Teller Machine (ATM),
    101

Bach, Johann Sebastian: *Mass in B
    Minor*, 259
Ball, Hugo, 297
Balzac, Honoré de: *Le Père Goriot*,
    141
Banister, Reverend John, 203
Baudelaire, Charles, 280; 'The
    Albatross', 292–3
Bell, Alexander Graham, 37
Beowulf, 97
Beverley, Robert, 203
Bierstadt, Albert: *Western
    Landscape* (painting), *254–5*
Bird, Alfred, 37
Blair, Robert: 'The Grave', 240
bohemians, bohemianism, 277–80,
    283–4, 287, 289, 293–5, 299–301
bourgeoisie: bohemian dislike
    of, 279; interest in wealth, 105;
    Marx on, 72–3, 106; self-interest,
    106
breastfeeding, 174, *176*
Bright, John, 133
Britain: industrial revolution, 35;
    land enclosures, 99; meritocracy
    in, 83–5
Browne, Sir Thomas: 'Urne-
    Buriall', 238–9
Bukowski, Charles: 'Something for
    the Touts, the Nuns, the Grocery
    Clerks and You' (poem), 283
Burckhardt, Jacob: *The Civilization
    of the Renaissance in Italy*, 222

businesses: executives' behaviour, 177–9

capitalism, 72, 198
Caricature, La (magazine), 168
caricature and cartoons, 168–9, 171, 174, *175*, 176–7
Carlyle, Thomas, 80–81; *Midas*, 211
Carnegie, Andrew, 89, *90*
cathedrals, 268, *269*, 270, *272–3*
Chamfort, Sébastien-Roch Nicolas, 119, 125
Champaigne, Philippe de: *Vanitas* (painting), *236*
Chardin, Jean-Baptiste: *Meal for a Convalescent* (painting), 145, *146*
charity, 89
Charivari, Le (magazine), 169
Chatterton, Thomas, 289, *290–91*
Chauncey, Henry, 82
Chesterfield, Philip Dormer Stanhope, 4th Earl of: *Letters to His Son*, 189
children, 258
China: dress, 102; status of farmers in, 22
Christianity: and acceptance of inequality, 48, 50; artistic achievements, 267–8; belief in individual worth and community, 257–61; and death, 229–31, 233, 239, 248; declining regard for, 106; influence, 226; and poverty, 70–71; saints, 188; and social status, 79, 263–4; spiritual values, 264, 267–8, 301; Tolstoy embraces, 230
Church, Frederic Edwin: *Niagara* (painting), *250–51*
cinema, 60

Civil Service (British), 83, 85
class (social): and democracy, 51–2; differences, 137–9; landed, 214; Marx on, 72–3; ruling, 214, 222; structure, 67–8
comedy, 167–8, 171–4, 180–82
commercial organizations: procedures, 107
communal relationships, 105, 257–60
company profits, 101–2
Conant, James, 82–3
conscience, 128
courage, 193
Courbet, Gustave: *Portrait of the Artist (Man with a Pipe)* (painting), *282*
creativity, 193
Cromer, Evelyn Baring, 1st Earl of, 213
Crosse & Blackwell (company), 37
Cubeo tribe (Brazil), 190
culture, 133–5
cynics, 128

Dadaism, 295, 297–8, 302
Daily Telegraph, 134, 211
dancing, 189
Dante Alighieri: *Divine Comedy*, 264
David, Jacques-Louis: *Le Sacre de Joséphine* (painting), 169, *170*
death, 229–35, 238, 248
decency, 196
deference, 21
Defoe, Daniel, 35
Delamare, Delphine (*née* Couturier), 163–4
democracies, 53–4
department stores, 35, *36*

dependence, 96–102
deprivation: perception of, 45
Deschamps, Eustache, 57
Diaz de Gamez, Gutierre: *The Unconquered Knight*, 189
dignity, 12
Diogenes, 119–20
disease, 34
dishonour *see* honour
Doré, Gustave: *The New Zealander* (engraving), 244, *245*; *The Thieves Tortured by Serpents* (engraving), *266*; *The Violent Tortured in the Rain of Fire* (engraving), *265*
Doulton (sanitary company), 37
Dryden, John, 174
Duchamp, Marcel, 280, 295
duelling, 115–17

Ecclesiastes, Book of, 235
economic imperative, 107
education: and merit, 82–3
egalitarianism, 81; *see also* inequalities
ego, 16
Eliot, George, 153; *Middlemarch*, 141, 143
Eluard, Paul, *276*
Emerson, Ralph Waldo, 80, 300; *Self-Reliance*, 294
Empedocles, 120
employers: dependence on, 97–102, 108
Engels, Friedrich: *The Condition of the Working-class in England*, 73
England: recognition of status in, 189–90
envy, 46–7, 52, 182, 208
Epictetus, 119
Epicurus, 195

Europe, Western: recognition of status in, 188–90
expectation, 55–6, 63

failure: fear of, 157–8
Fallows, Samuel: *The Problem of Success for Young Men and How to Solve It*, 58
fame, 11
fashion, 35
fiction *see* novels
Fidelin, Ady, *276*
flattery, 23–5
Flaubert, Gustave, 279; *Madame Bovary*, 164–5; *Salammbô*, 294
Fortescue, Sir John, 50, 54
Fouché, Joseph, 171
France: Napoleonic reforms, 80
Franklin, Benjamin: *Autobiography*, 58
Freedley, Edwin T.: *The Secret of Success in Life*, 58
Freud, Sigmund: *The Joke and Its Relation to the Unconscious*, 173
Fruitlands, Massachusetts, 300
furniture, 28

Galbraith, John Kenneth: *The Affluent Society*, 196
Gandy, Joseph: *View of the Rotunda of the Bank of England in Ruins* (painting), 240, *242–3*
gentlemen, 189–90
Gerard, Bishop of Cambrai, 69
Gibbon, Edward: *Decline and Fall of the Roman Empire*, 204
Gillray, James: *The Grand Coronation Procession of Napoleone* (cartoon), 169, 171, *172–3*

global economy, 102–4
Goethe, Johann Wolfgang von, 244, 294
golden mean, 123
Graveyard School (of poets), 239
Gray, Thomas: 'Elegy Written in a Country Churchyard', 240
Greeks, ancient, 96, 119, 158
Greenwich Village, 295
Guicciardini, Francesco, 100
Gursky, Andreas, 42–3

Hall, Bolton: *Three Acres and Liberty*, 98
hamartia (lapse of judgement), 159, 162
happiness: and acquisition/achievement, 207–8; and making money, 200–201
Hardy, Thomas: *Jude the Obscure*, 141
Harmsworth, Alfred (Viscount Northcliffe), 60
Harrison, Frederic, 133
heaven and hell, 264, 265
hell *see* heaven and hell
Herbert, Edward, 1st Baron Herbert of Cherbury, 115
hereditary principle, 79–80
Herodotus, 231, 233
hierarchy, 48, 49, 50–54, 140, 302–3
Hobbes, Thomas: *Leviathan*, 50
honour, 115–17, 120–22, 192
Hoover vacuum cleaners, 39
Howard, Brian, 278–9
Hugo, Victor: *Hernani*, 293–4
human imperative, 107
Hume, David: *Of Luxury*, 76; *A Treatise on Human Nature*, 47
humour, 171, 177–81; *see also* comedy

Hunt, Reverend Thomas P.: *The Book of Wealth*, 85–6

ideology, 214, 218, 222
Image du Monde, 68
Indians (native American), 202–4
individualism, 257, 260–1, 293–4
inequalities, 46–51, 53; *see also* egalitarianism
influence, 11
insignificance, sense of, 249
intelligence, 193, 197–8
inventions, 37

Jackson & Graham (furniture manufacturers), 28, 29
Jacobello de Fiore: *The Coronation of the Virgin in Paradise* (painting), 49
James I, King of England, 172
James, William, 55–6, 63; *The Principles of Psychology*, 15
Japan: dress, 102
Jefferson, Thomas, 52
Jennings, George, 37, 38
Jesus Christ, 70, 79, 188, 199, 226, 257, 263; *see also* Christianity
John de Grailly, 188
John of Salisbury, Bishop of Chartres: *Policraticus*, 50, 54
Johnson, Samuel, 174
jokes, 173
Jolly-Bellin (Paris tailor), 37
Jones, Thomas: *Buildings in Naples*, 147, 150; *Rooftops, Naples*, 147–8, 148–9
Josephine, Empress of Napoleon, 169, 170, 171

Kant, Immanuel: *Groundwork of the Metaphysic of Morals*, 106

Kellogg, J.H., 37
Kennedy, John F., 84
Kerouac, Jack, 280
Khrushchev, Nikita S., *32*, 33–4
knights, 188–9
Købke, Christen, 148–50, 153; *The Roof of Frederiksborg Castle* (painting), *152*; *View from the Embankment of Lake Sortedam* (painting), *151*; *A View in the Neighbourhood of the Lime Kiln* (painting), *154–5*

labour: and capital, 107–8; dependence on employers, 97–102, 108; division of, 61; Marx on, 72–3; *see also* employers; poverty
La Bruyère, Jean de, 100
landscape, 249, *250–55*
La Rochefoucauld, François, 6th Duc de, 100
Lawrence, William, Bishop of Massachusetts, 86
Legion of Honour, 80
Lenin, Vladimir, 210
Leonardo da Vinci: *Mona Lisa* (painting), 295, *296*
Lesueur, Jean-François, 169
Limbourg Brothers: *Peasants at Work on a Feudal Estate* (painting), *70*
living standards, 34
Locke, John: *Two Treatises of Government*, 51
Lodoiska, Countess, 115
loneliness, 128
Louis-Philippe, King of France, 167–8, 171
love: absence of, 15, 17; as aim of

high status, 11, 13–14, 16–17; and the dying, 231, 233; and employment conditions, 108; need for, 109, 258; unconditional, 23, 122
luck, 96–7
Luke, St, 263, 267
luxury, 76

Machiavelli, Niccolò, 100
Maher, William: *On the Road to Riches*, 58
Mandeville, Bernard: *The Fable of the Bees*, 75–6
Marcus Aurelius: *Meditations*, 121–2
Marinetti, Filippo: *The Futurist Cookbook*, 298–9
Marvell, Andrew: 'To His Coy Mistress', 232
Marx, Karl: on class, 72–3, 106; on ideology, 214; Shaw on, 210; *Capital*, 72, 85; *The Communist Manifesto* (with Engels), 73, 106
Marxism: and rise of industrial proletariat, 99
mass media, 60–1
material progress, 33–5, 37–40, 45
Mathews, William: *Getting on in the World*, 58
merit: as basis for status, 51–2, 79, 81–6, 89, 197–8; *see also* virtue
Miller, Lee, *288*; *Le Déjeuner sur l'Herbe* (photograph), *276*
misanthropy, intelligent, 125–9
money *see* wealth
Montaigne, Michel de, 199–200
Moran, Thomas: *Nearing Camp, Evening on the Upper Colorado River, Wyoming* (painting), *252–3*
Morse, Jedidiah, 51

Murger, Henri: *Scènes de la vie de Bohème*, 277
Muses, Nine, 96

Nägeli, Hans-Georg, 259
Napoleon I (Bonaparte), Emperor of the French, 80, 169, 171
natural ideas, 213–15
needs, 201–2, 205
neglect (social), 17
nepotism, 84
Nerval, Gérard de, 289, 292, 294, 298
New Yorker (magazine), 177
newspapers, 25–6, 60, 157–8
Nixon, Richard M., *32*, 33–4, 45
nobodies, 12; *see also* insignificance
Northcliffe, Viscount *see* Harmsworth, Alfred
Northcote, Sir Stafford, 83
novels (fiction), 140–44
Nusch (model), *276*

Oedipus, King of Thebes, 160–63
ordinariness, 257–8
Orwell, George: *The Lion and the Unicorn*, 40, 84

Paine, Tom: *The Rights of Man*, 80
paintings, 145–50
paternalism, 69
peasantry, 67–9, *68*, 69–70, *69*, *70*
Penrose, Roland, *276*
Percy, Henry George, Earl, 213
Périer, Casimir, 167
Philip the Good, Duke of Burgundy, 57
Philipon, Charles, 168, 172
Pius VII, Pope, 169, 171
Poe, Edgar Allan, 292

Portrait of an Artist in his Studio (painting; artist unknown), *281*
poverty and the poor: class values, 67–9; declining respect for, 106; deserved, 86–8, 91; Engels on, 73; and goodness, 264; and material progress, 34; and shame, 196–7; in USA, 34, 54; as wealth producers, 69, 75
power: and snobs, 22
pretentiousness, 56, 174, 176–7
pride, 76
Priestley, J.B.: *English Journey*, 38
progress, 35
property: as theft, 71–2
Proust, Marcel, 147; *In Search of Lost Time*, 24
public opinion, 125–9
Pullars of Perth (dry-cleaners), 37
Punch (magazine), 26–7, 176, *177*

race, 213–14; *see also* Indians (native American); savages
radio, 60–61
Ramm, Tanja, *288*
Ramsay, David: *Oration on the Advantages of American Independence*, 51
Ramses II, Pharaoh, 244
Ransome, Arthur: *Bohemia in London*, 277
Ray, Man, *276*
reason, 121–3
respect, 21, 126
rich, the: as morally deserving, 85–7; and privilege, 71–4; social usefulness, 75–8; *see also* wealth
Richter, Hans, 298
Robbins, Anthony: *Awaken the Giant Within*, 58, *59*, 60

Robert, Hubert ('Robert des Ruines'), 240; *Imaginary View of the Grande Gallerie of the Louvre in Ruins* (painting), *241*
Roberts, David: *Doorway at Baalbec* (painting), *247*; *General View of Baalbec* (painting), *246*
Rockefeller, John D., 86
Rome: Renaissance, 22
Roosevelt, Franklin D., 40
Ropp, Baron von, 115
Rosenplüt, Hans, 69
Rousseau, Jean-Jacques: *Discourse on the Origin of Inequality*, 62–3, 71–2, 85, 201–2, 204
ruins, 240, *241*–3, 244, *245*–7, 248–9
Ruskin, John, 209–11; *Unto This Last*, 199, 209

Saint-André, Simon Renard de: *Vanitas*, *236*
saints (Christian), 188
SAT system (USA), 82–3, 85
satire, 174
savages, 61–3, 202
Schopenhauer, Arthur: *Parerga and Paralipomena*, 119, 127–9
Sears Catalogue, 40, *41*
self-esteem, 12, 55–6, 67, 126–7, 195
self-image, 116, 120–21
self-interest, 105–6
Selfridge, Gordon, 35
servants, 54
Shakespeare, William, 232–3
Shaw, George Bernard: on Ruskin, 210; *The Intelligent Woman's Guide to Socialism and Capitalism*, 198–9, 215
Shelley, Percy Bysshe: 'Ozymandias', 244

Singer, I.M., 37
slavery, 48
Smiles, Samuel: *Self-help*, 88
Smith, Adam: *Inquiry into the Nature and Causes of the Wealth of Nations*, 61, 77, 105, 195–7; *The Theory of Moral Sentiments*, 13
Smith, Zadie: *White Teeth*, 144
snobbery: defined, 21–2; and flattery, 23–4; and social scorn, 26–8
Social Darwinism, 87–8
society: compared to body, 50
Socrates, 119–20
somebodies, 12
Sophocles: *Oedipus the King*, 160–62
space, 249
Sparta, Spartans, 22, 187–8, 190
Speer, William: *The Law of Success*, 58
Spencer, Herbert: *Social Statics*, 88
stamina, 193
status: basis for, 51; defined, 3; hunger for, 5; moral connotations, 79; requirements of, 187–93
status anxiety: defined, 3–5, 302; perception of, 45–6
status symbols, 197
Stendhal (Marie-Henri Beyle), 279; *On Love*, 283; *Promenades dans Rome*, 244
Stephens, Alexander, 214
success: attainment of, 58–60, 86
suicide, 53
Suicide Club (Paris), 294–5
Surrealism, 298, 302

talent: fickle, 96
television, 60–61
Thackeray, William Makepeace: on newspapers, 25–6; *Book of Snobs*, 21–2, 25
Theresa of Avila, St, 141, 143
Thoreau, Henry David, 284–5, 287; *Walden*, 286
Tocqueville, Alexis de: *Democracy in America*, 52–5
Tolstoy, Count Leo: embraces Christianity, 230; *A Confession*, 229; *The Death of Ivan Ilyich*, 227–9
tradition, 126
tragedy, 157–63, 165
Trautmansdorf, Baron von, 115
Trevelyan, Sir Charles, 83
Twain, Mark: *Life on the Mississippi*, 37
Tzara, Tristan, 295

unemployment, 194
unhappiness, 57
United States of America: Christian morality in, 85–6; gross domestic product (1890–2000), 104; material progress, 33–4, 40; meritocracy in, 82–5; social status in, 51–4
Universal Declaration of Human Rights, 83

vanitas art, 235

Veblen, Thorstein: *The Theory of the Leisure Class*, 194–5
Vigny, Alfred de: *Chatterton*, 289
virtue, 194–9
Voltaire, François Marie Arouet, 127

Wallis, Henry: *The Death of Chatterton* (painting), 290–91
wealth: acquisition of, 11, 61; Christian justification for, 85–6; creation of, 74–8; and decency, 196; and happiness, 200–1; life as, 209–10; longing for, 62, 209; as sign of status, 193–4; and virtue, 194–5, 197–9; *see also* poverty; rich, the
Weber, Max, 222
Weimar: poets in, 22
Whitman, Walt: *Leaves of Grass*, 52
women: rights, 216–18; social status, 190, 213, 216
Woolf, Virginia: 216, 218; and women's rights, 216–18; *A Room of One's Own*
workers *see* labour

Xerxes, King of Persia, 233

Young, Edward: 'Night Thoughts', 239–40
Young, Michael: *The Rise of Meritocracy*, 91

Zurich, 260